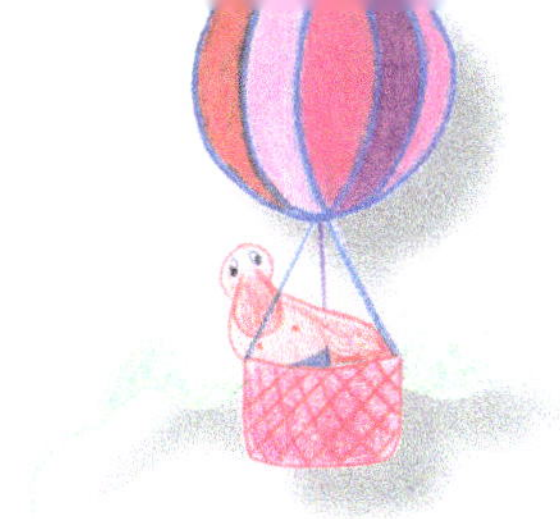

DO YOUR WORLD DIFFERENTLY

365 ways to shake up your life

Louise Siversen and Georgina Capper

Do Your World Differently
365 ways to shake up your life

ISBN 978-0-6454302-0-2

For the love of doing.

To adventures large and small.

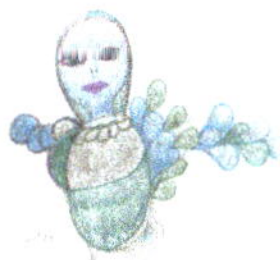

WHAT IS THIS?

This book presents an adventure.
Made up of 365 tiny adventures.
One tiny call to action for each day of a year.
One tiny call to action that will create an incremental expansion of your perception,
and with it your capacity for so much more.

SO WHO'S IT FOR?

- anyone wanting to expand their world and their perception of it, or
- anyone who wants to find or expand their creative self, or
- anyone who feels like they need to begin a new chapter, or
- anyone who is starting to wrestle with the feeling that their life might be possibly maybe conceivably turning somewhat slightly vaguely beige, or
- anyone who is curious about what might happen if…

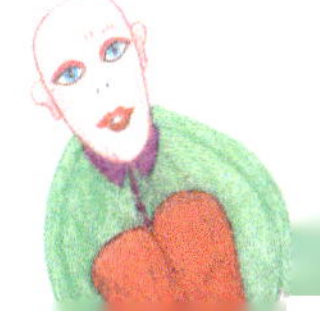

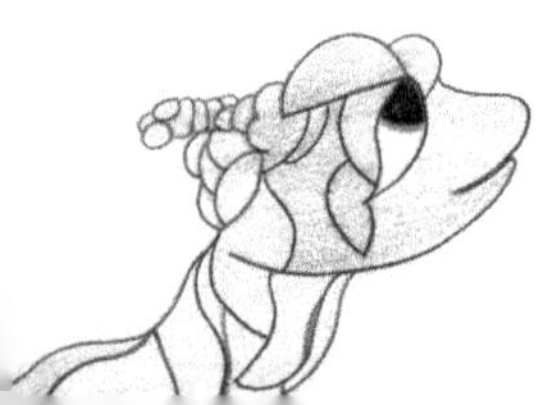

OKAY I'M LISTENING...

We give so much of ourselves, our time, our focus to other people. Often we fill our lives with others and their destinies and dreams and dramas, and we forget to make time for ourselves.

This book makes you your priority. Just for a couple of minutes a day it lets you and your mind, body, imagination, breath become your focus. And in doing so you can start to create a practice that will shift you towards the things that are important to you.

The only thing that you have to do each day is choose to pick up the book and follow the day's prompt. That's it. Easy.

Ultimately this book offers you a yearlong experiment as a means by which you can entertain new ways of being. It will either appeal to you or it won't. It will resonate with something deep in you – or you'll feel nothing. Take it or leave it. Both are perfect.

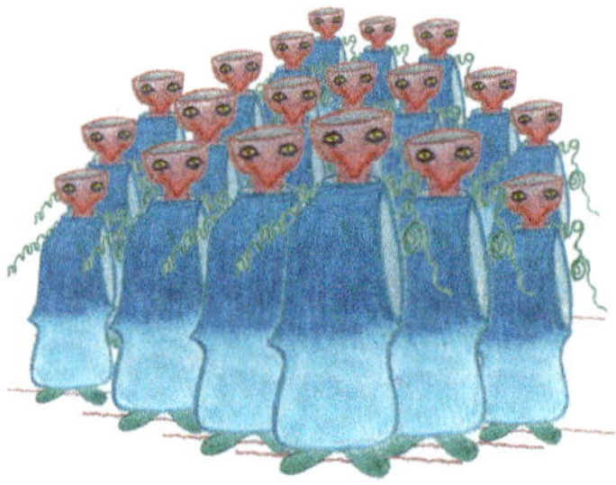

BUT I DON'T KNOW WHAT I'M DOING!

Who does?! Let's just – go for it!

We didn't know what we were doing when we made this book. But we made a book. That was our experiment. And we began it by beginning.

Travel beyond your borders! See the land stretching out in front of you, urging you to take up space and time for new and exciting endeavours.

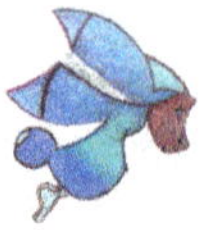

We appreciate that everyone's physical/living/working situations are different.

If there's a reason that a task is unachievable then simply modify to accommodate what is doable for you right now.

Allow your inventiveness to enrich this very personal experience, without losing any challenge that may enable expansive change.

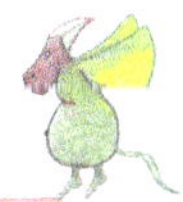

BREATHE

Each week, the first task asks you to observe your breath. It is the only task for that day, and its repetition is expected each day for the rest of the week.

To observe your breath, simply follow it in and out of the body. If you lose your concentration simply return to the next breath and start again.

→ Pay attention → Lose concentration → Return to breath → Repeat →

If you are comfortable to do so, we recommend gently closing your eyes while you observe your breath. It can offer you a deeper experience, relieving you of external stimulus and helping your focus to remain on your inhalation and exhalation.

We also encourage silence during this time. Nothing nurtures creativity like the chance to regroup and rest in the infinite nature of our own selves - it is a non-negotiable for change.

WHY THESE IMAGES?

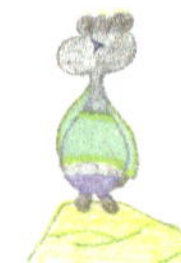

Louise says: Every year I choose to learn a new skill. I do it for many reasons, mostly because I love learning, but also because being in a world of "I don't know" helps me to expand my borders.

In 2016 I decided to learn how to draw. I drew for 365 days to see what would happen.

In the beginning the drawings were incomprehensible - a splotchy mess. But as the weeks and months passed I became more proficient. Why? Because I practised every day. I up-skilled via my effort.

When I began I drew hoping inspiration would strike. I soon realised I needed to cultivate a more meaningful relationship to the act of drawing. So I provided myself with a prompt, an intention by reading inspiring text after my morning meditation.

It could be any subject: poetry, prose, philosophy, neuroscience, politics, history, art, literature, business, fashion - anything that took my attention.

I then extracted a single sentence that encapsulated the theme of my reading. I wrote that sentence on the page in my sketch book where I intended to draw, then I allowed a stream of consciousness to unfold imaginatively, drawing over the words. Slowly a picture would emerge and I discovered what lay within the words and my experience of them.

The fifty-two drawings within this book are all from my 2016 experiment. They are not perfect images and they are not trying to be. They are an expression of my journey on a single day in 2016. What I learned, what I enjoyed, how I unfolded through the process of participation.

"They are not perfect images and they are not trying to be."

This book grew out of these images and the notion that we can gain pleasure from the things we produce with our imaginations.

In 2020 I decided my year long experiment would be a to make a book that encouraged others to explore their creativity. I wanted to share the experience with my dear friend Georgina so together we pooled our creative resources and taught ourselves how to make a book - our way. We learned a lot - not all of it about how to make a book!

This creative adventure will unquestionably alter your point of view by engaging you with new content and ideas, and that alone might just lead you to something surprising and energising.

You might just do your world differently.

HOW THIS BOOK?

Georgina says: Louise approached me with an idea: to make a book. Okay, I said, let's do it. I had no idea how to make one and neither did Louise. So we met and drank tea and discussed the possibilities, and soon realised we already had several elements in our favour: an idea, the illustrations, a basic knowledge of some design software, an understanding of story arc, the capacity to take feedback, and a willingness to work. Excellent, we thought.

And not sure how to begin we began.

> *"...the most essential feature of this book is the fact that we made it ourselves."*

We spent a lot of time learning just how much we didn't know. When we didn't know something we used a search engine. Or asked. Or guessed. We created according to our shared knowledge, our shared aesthetic. We fed back, we accepted feedback, we made mistakes, we started again, we started again again, we shared meals, we skyped, we brainstormed – our discussions were highlights.

Without a shred of doubt the most essential feature of this book is the fact that we made it ourselves.

Normally we would ask a book expert to make our book, as we are all for expertise. But this concept is not about two book experts putting together a book. It is about doing. It is about expanding our experience, opening ourselves to discomfort, being consistent - sometimes during heartache, illness, anxiety, Covid, separated by a Ring Of Steel for much of the time for goodness' sake. Working when we didn't feel like it. Just getting on with it. Doing.

Our lack of experience was the point. Our learning was the point. Our setting our minds to one tiny task at a time and doing it was the point.

The aim of this book is not to teach you how to make your own book. You may well feel compelled to make one. You might end up making a whole series. Or you might start taking photos, or reading more often, or noticing flowers open and close. You might begin to feel a spark of excitement as you take back some time for you. Or you may simply enjoy the challenge of committing to something that demands of you as much or as little time as you can give to focus on doing.

For us it was essential to espouse this ideal. To present these prompts in a small square book that we made ourselves simply by doing it.

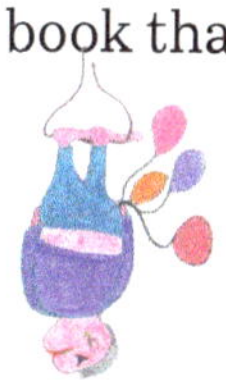

ASTERISKS

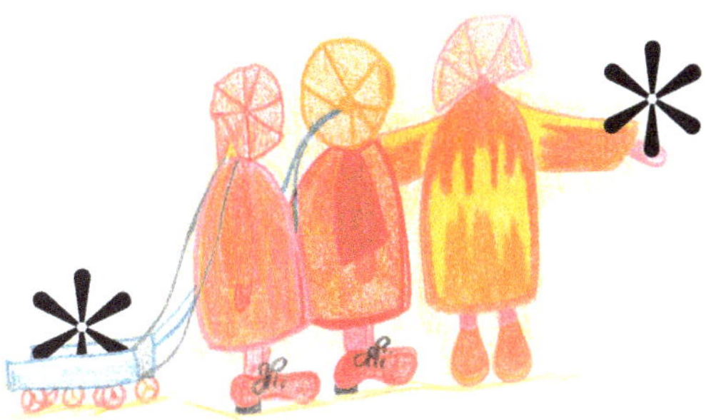

**An asterisk lets you know that*

there's more information at

the back of the book...

PART ONE

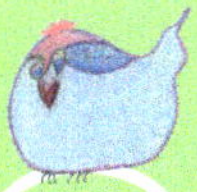

Pay Attention

1. Observe your breath for 1 minute for 7 days. Witness the full inhale and the full exhale.

2. Photograph something you have never seen before. Really take your time.

3. Choose a jubilant song. Sing for 10 minutes. Record for posterity.

4. Alter the placement of 7 items in your home. Stand back, behold the impact.

5. Listen to the pauses in your heart beat. Do you need to pause today?

6. Are you splitting your attention? Take action with specificity and patience today.

7. Place pen/pencil and journal next to your bed for use in coming weeks.

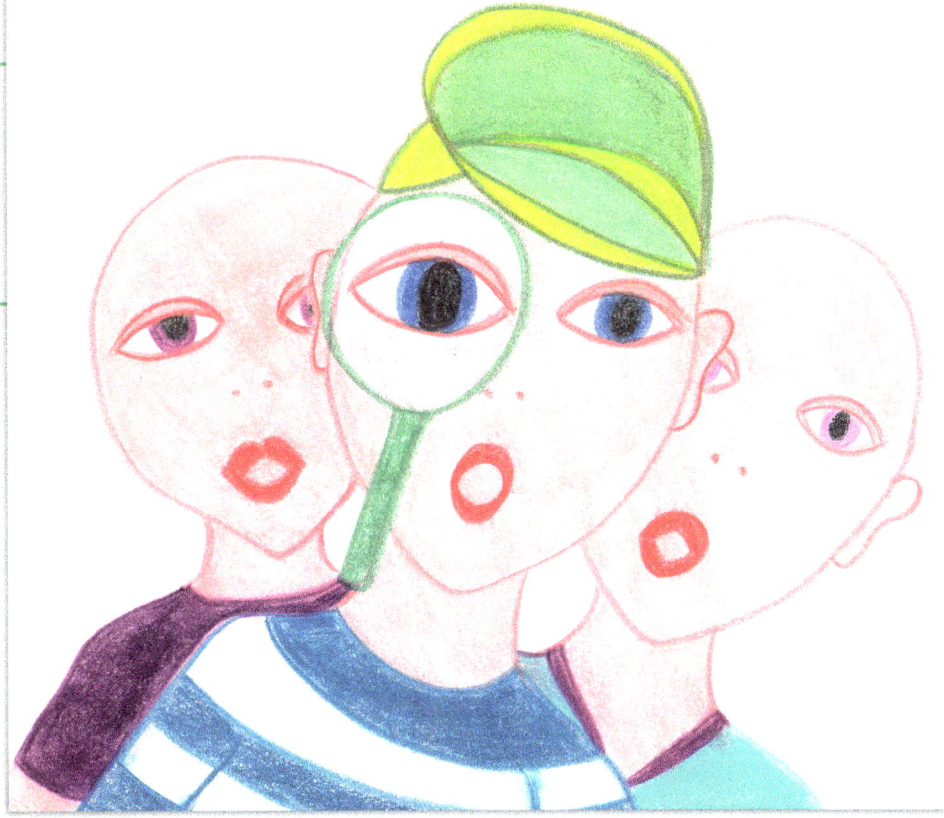

Be Curious

1. Observe your breath for 1 minute each day for 7 days. Just for one minute be here now.

2. List 3 books in your journal that you want to read. Access one to begin today.

3. What question lies at the heart of your life? Journal answer.

4. Write a paragraph in your journal describing something you don't understand.

5. What are the measurements of the Sun? Journal discoveries.

6. Research 1 new fact on 7 different topics today. What interested you?

7. Prepare an art kit. Paints, pencils, paper, scissors, paste etc. You are now ready to make art.

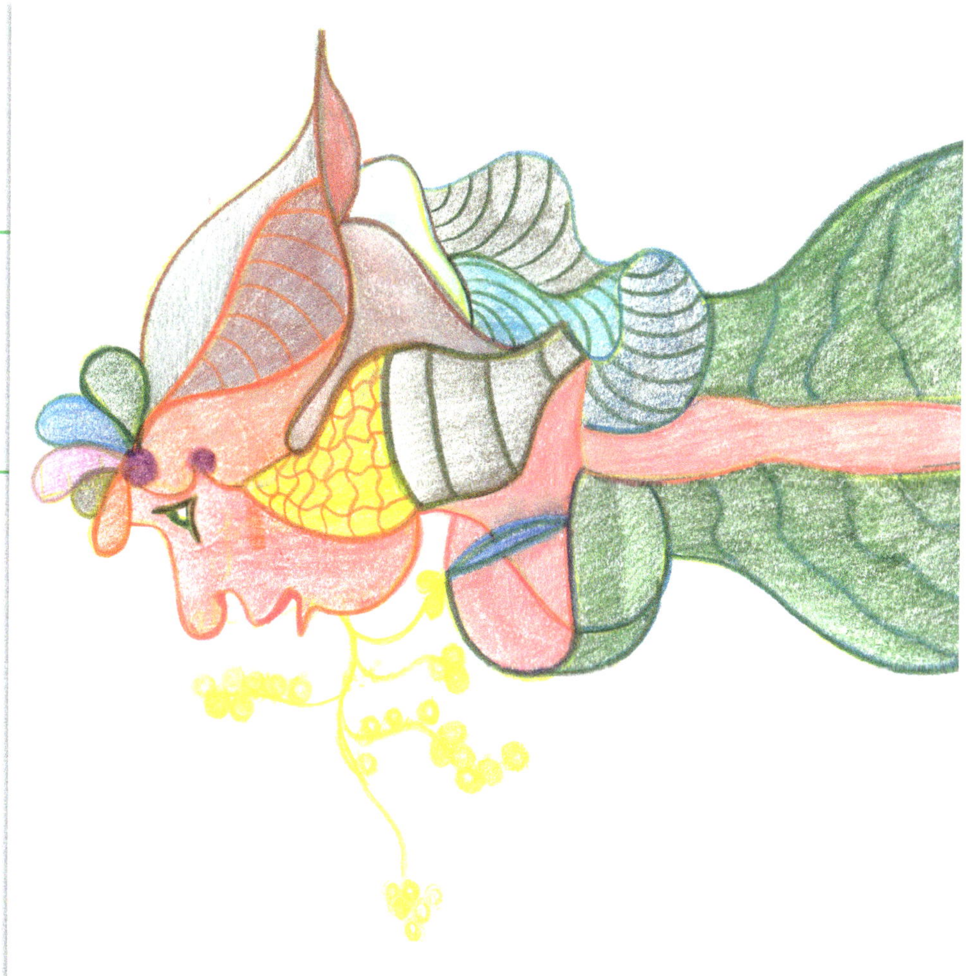

Seek Purpose

1. Observe your breath for 1 minute each day for 7 days. Seated.
2. Locate a memory of yourself as a child. What do you recognise? And what is forgotten?*
3. Complete 2 tasks today that you have been delaying. Go.
4. Commit an act of kindness for yourself before midday today. Relish the love.
5. Journal 5 values essential for your well being. Institute them with generosity today.
6. Make 3 informed decisions today to benefit your future self. Be your greatest ally.
7. Discover a new poem. How does it speak to you? Read out loud filled with this intent.

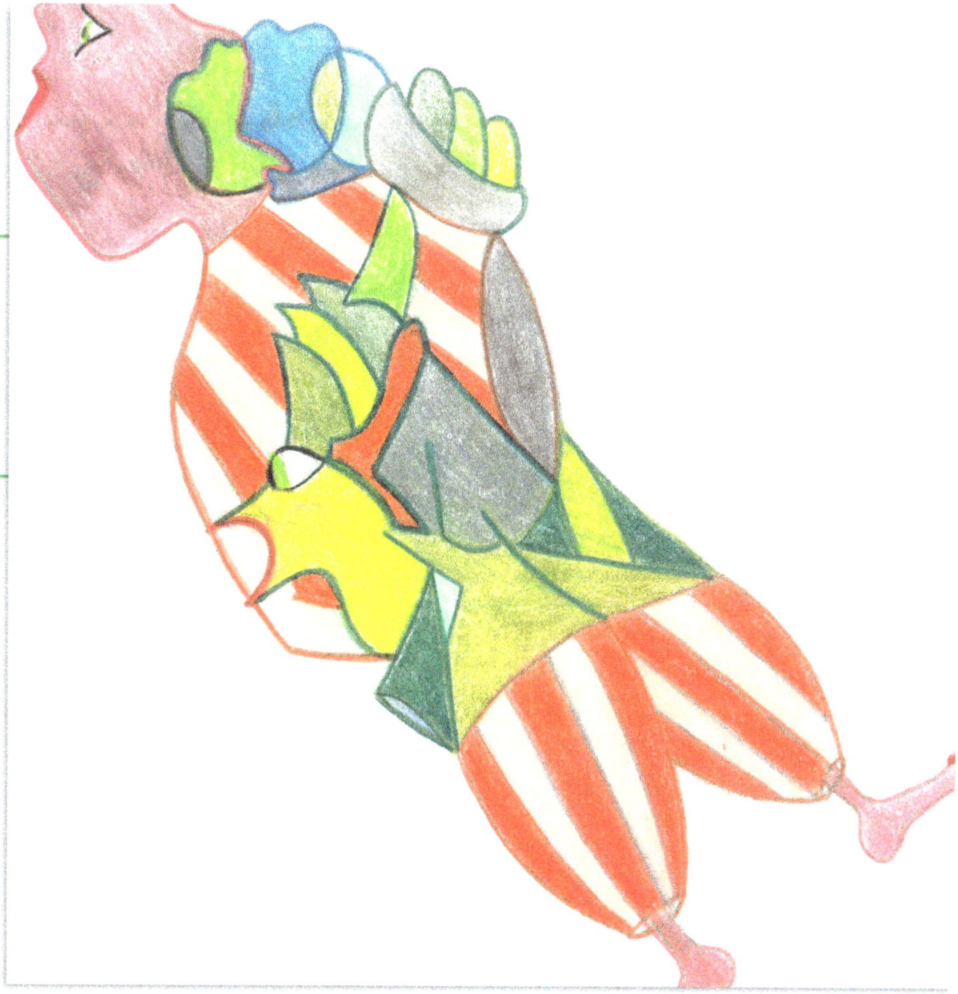

Foster Will Power

1. Observe your breath for 2 minutes a day for 7 days. Be aware of body sensations.

2. Deliberately interrupt your routine. SHAKE IT TO THE CORE.

3. Exercise for 20 minutes. Rejoice in the movement large or small.

4. Refrain from sugar for 24 hours. Journal any consequences.

5. Take the stairs. Go.*

6. Stay off all devices for 2 hours today. Experiment creatively with time.*

7. Practice your art, yes YOUR art. Draw, paint, write, collage... welcome inspiration.

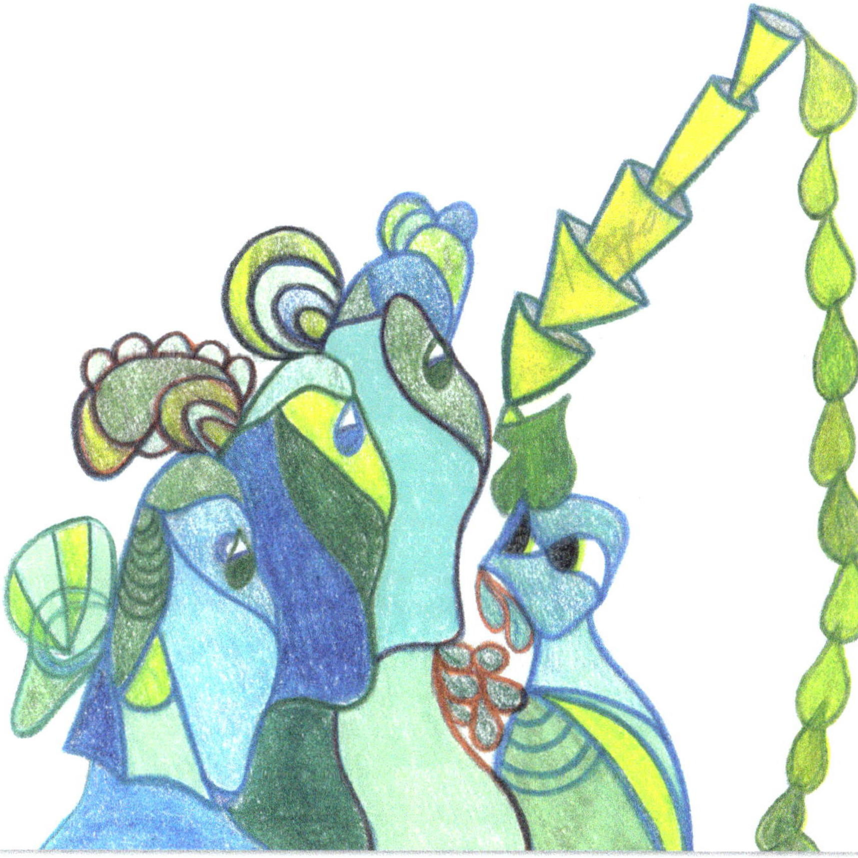

28 WEEK FIVE

Work

1. Observe your breath for 2 minutes a day for 7 days. Seated. Remain completely still.

2. List tasks to accomplish this week in order of priority. Giddy up.

3. What do you want to improve? Then practice it for 20 minutes each day.

4. List every item you bought in the last 24 hours. Did you need it? Really?

5. Say “no” to pressures that waste your time and energy today. What changes?

6. Create an opportunity for yourself today. Be flamboyant. Take up space.

7. Refrain from complaint. Offer a solution instead. What shifts?

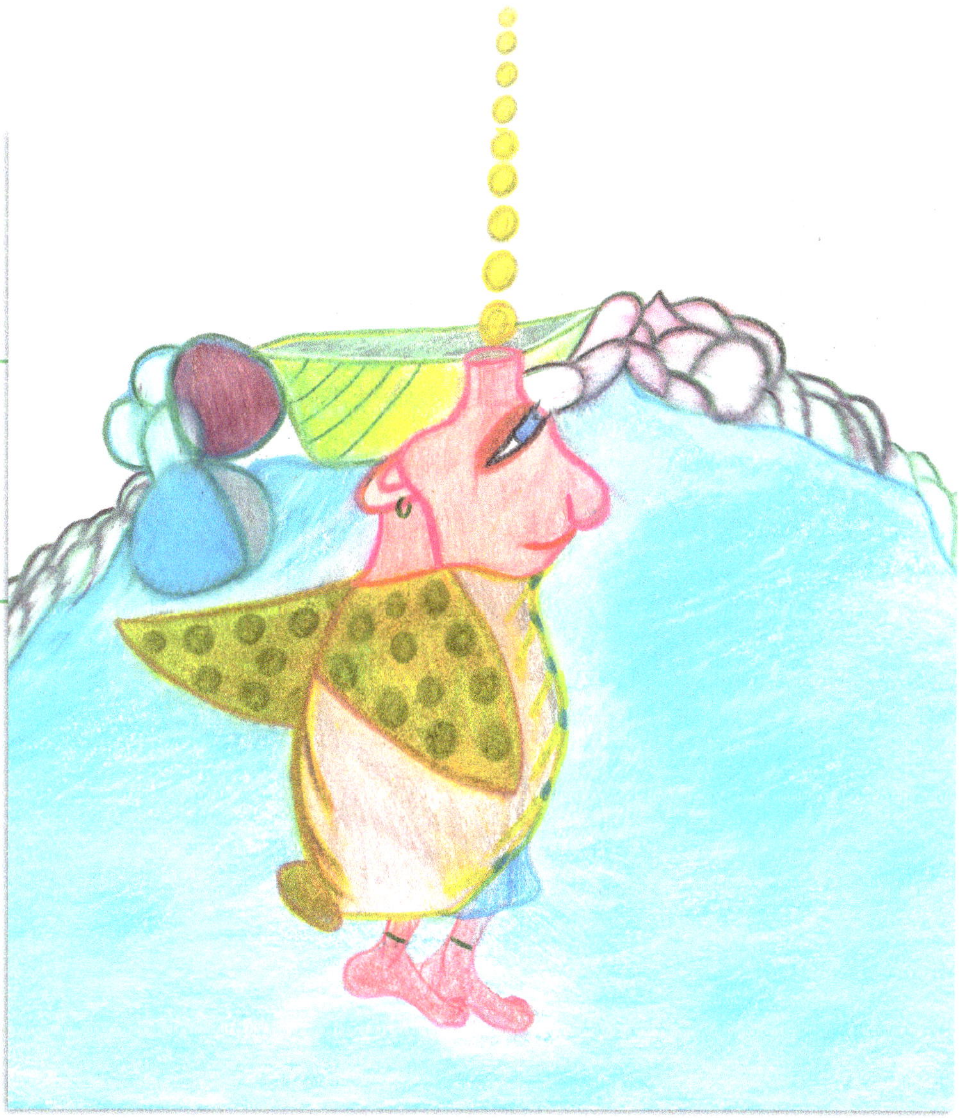

30 WEEK SIX

Welcome Change

1. Observe your breath for 2 minutes a day for 7 days. Pause and witness your internal space.
2. Eat one new healthy food today.
3. Draw your ideal day. Be as radical or as abstract as you wish. Pin it up.
4. Clear your wardrobe of unwanted clothing. Let it go. Come on - let it go!
5. Well-being is realised in small steps. Take small steps today. Ask for help.
6. Go to bed an hour earlier and rest. Light off. Observe your breath.
7. Take a cold shower. Feel your body vibrate. Whoa!

Have you started on those books from Week 2 #2 yet? Just checking...

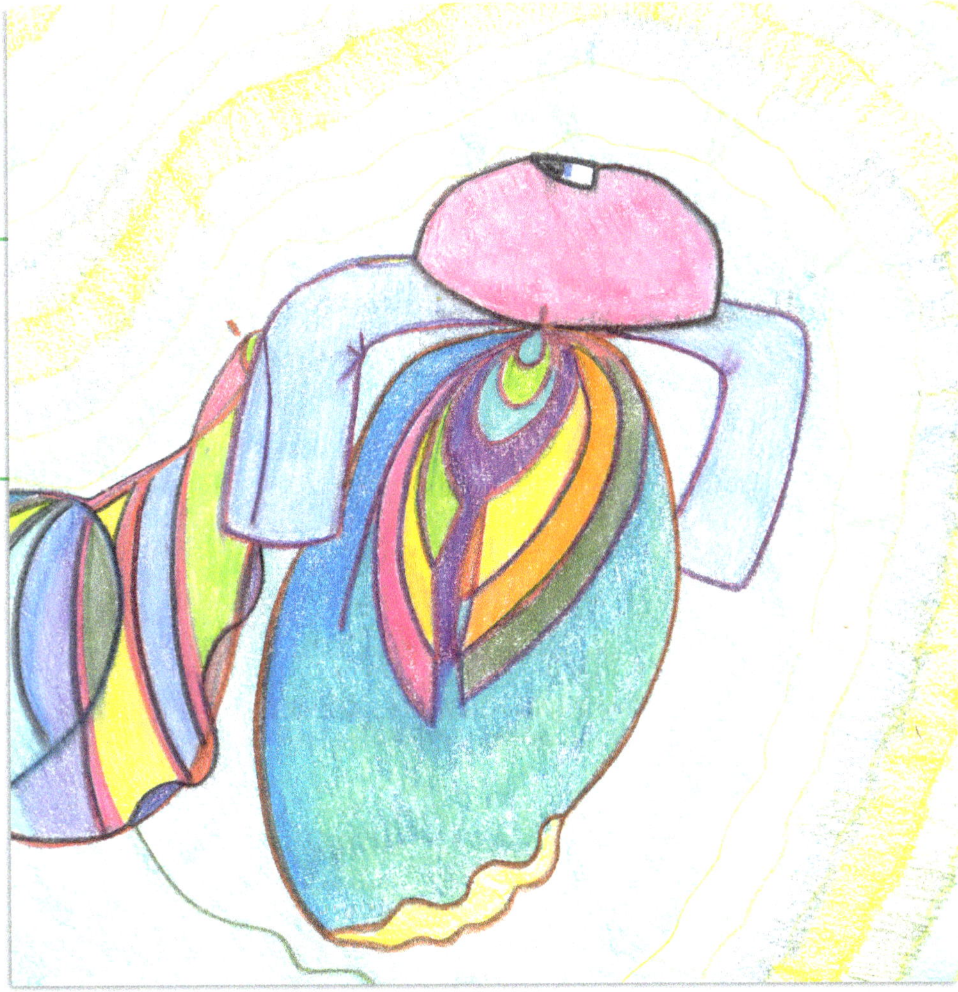

32 WEEK SEVEN

Reside in Reverence

1. Observe your breath for 2 minutes a day for 7 days. Is your breath hot or cold?
2. Go in to nature. Sit or lie down and receive the energy. Genuinely stop.
3. Write a hand-written note to someone who has helped you. Send.
4. When were you last humbled by mystery? Where? Why? Journal.
5. Visit a building that creates a sense of awe and wonder in you. What a miracle, eh?
6. Recall a teacher who influenced you. How have they shaped your life?
7. Reflect on your place in the Universe. It is home. How can you help protect it?

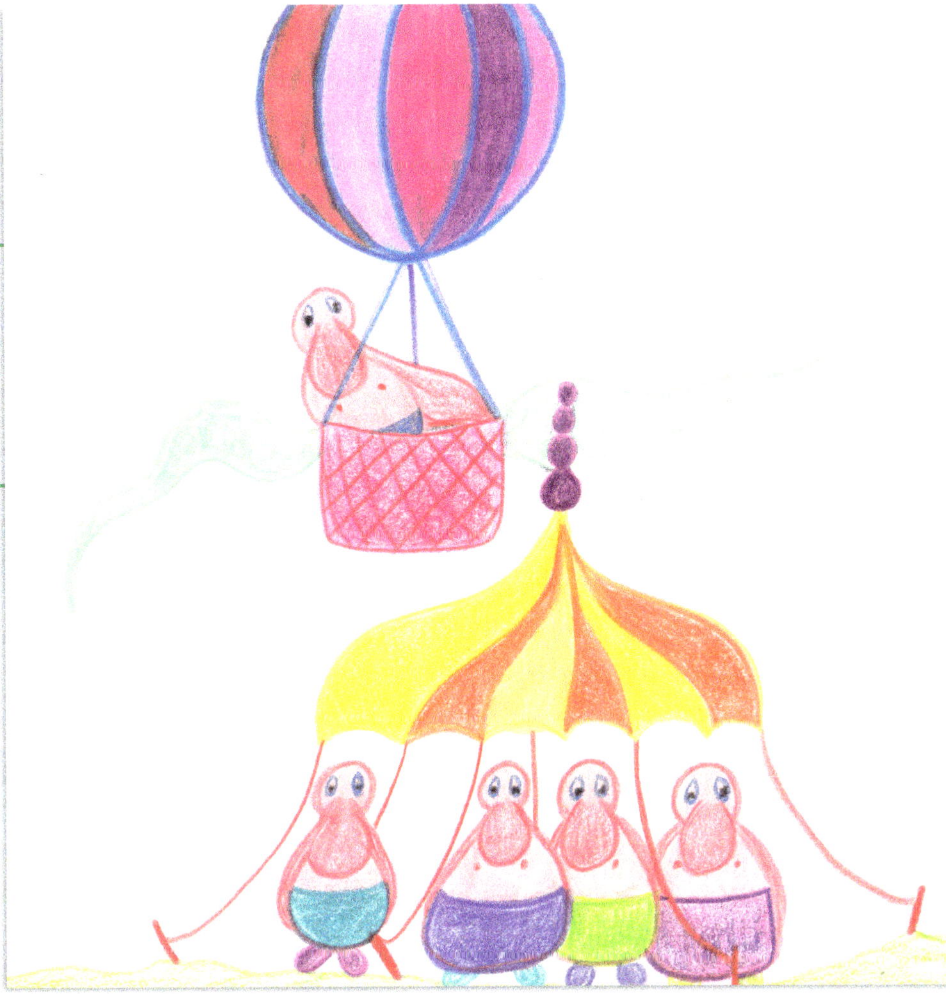

Be Kind [it's that simple]

1. Observe your breath for 3 minutes a day for 7 days. Can you deepen each breath?

2. Do you engage in gossip? Why? Cease.

3. Go out and play like a child today. Untether yourself.

4. How can you offer more loving compassion... to you? Do it right now.

5. Volunteer.

6. Massage your own feet. Close your eyes and connect to you. Hello!

7. Mail a hand written card of encouragement to yourself.

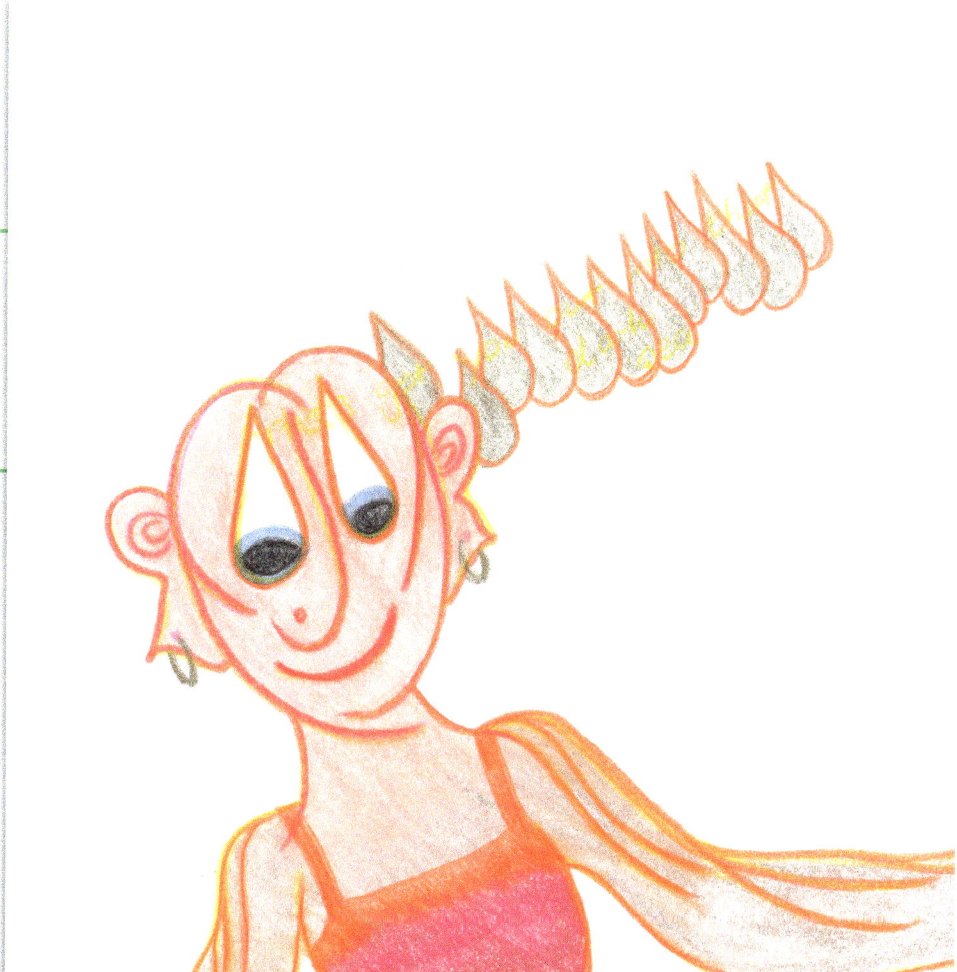

Move

1. Observe your breath for 3 minutes for 7 days. Feel your body expand and contract.
2. Walk for pleasure for 20 minutes. Photograph your journey in stages.
3. Dance... in your underwear. Shake it people!
4. Listen to music blindfolded for 20 minutes. Let resonance fill your body.
5. Draw your experience of joy. What colours do you need?
6. How do your legs move? Don't know? Find out.
7. Watch ants or bees or butterflies or birds and consider the miracle.

How is
Week 5 #3 going?
You can always start again,
you know...

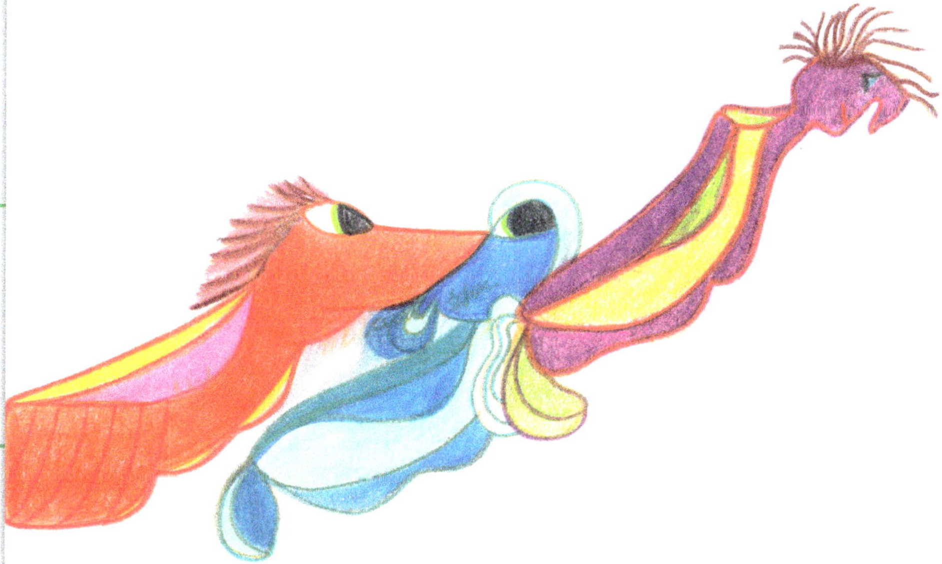

38 WEEK TEN

En-joy

1. Observe your breath for 3 minutes for 7 days. Wear a hat.

2. Watch 3 comedy films. Laugh out loud. Record your laughter. Listen.

3. Breathe one long inhale through your nose, exhale panting the word 'HUH'.

4. Walk down a hill and breathe the air with mouth open and tongue out.

5. Photograph what happiness looks like for you. Surprised?

6. Eat your favourite food for breakfast.

7. Find a playground and go on a swing. Swing high.*

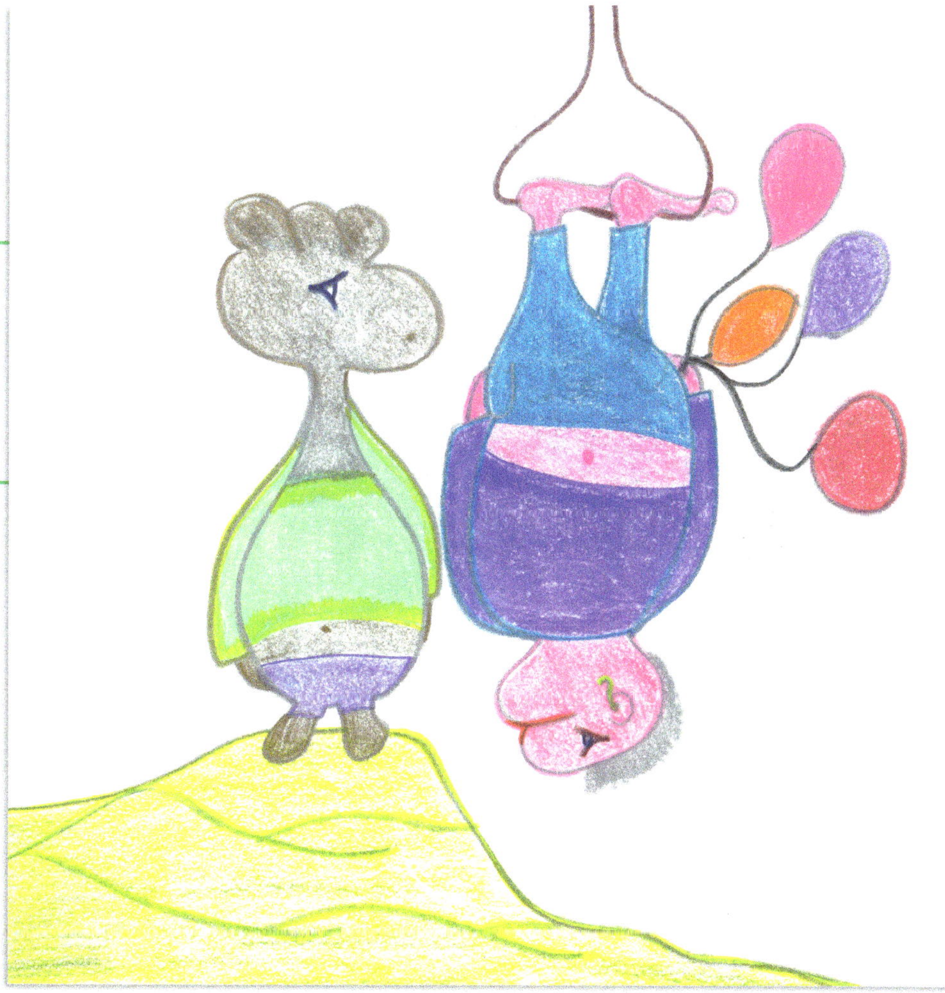

WEEK ELEVEN

Be Yourself

1. Observe your breath for 3 minutes for 7 days. Posture of choice.

2. Draw your potential. Pin it up. Now act on it.

3. What do you need to hear right now? Write it down in your journal in bold letters.

4. Do your clothes represent your true persona? No? Then change them.

5. You are your sole custodian. Are you helping? If not, why not?

6. With whom are you associating? Do they reflect your values?

7. Write a new poem inspired by your question from Week 2 #3.

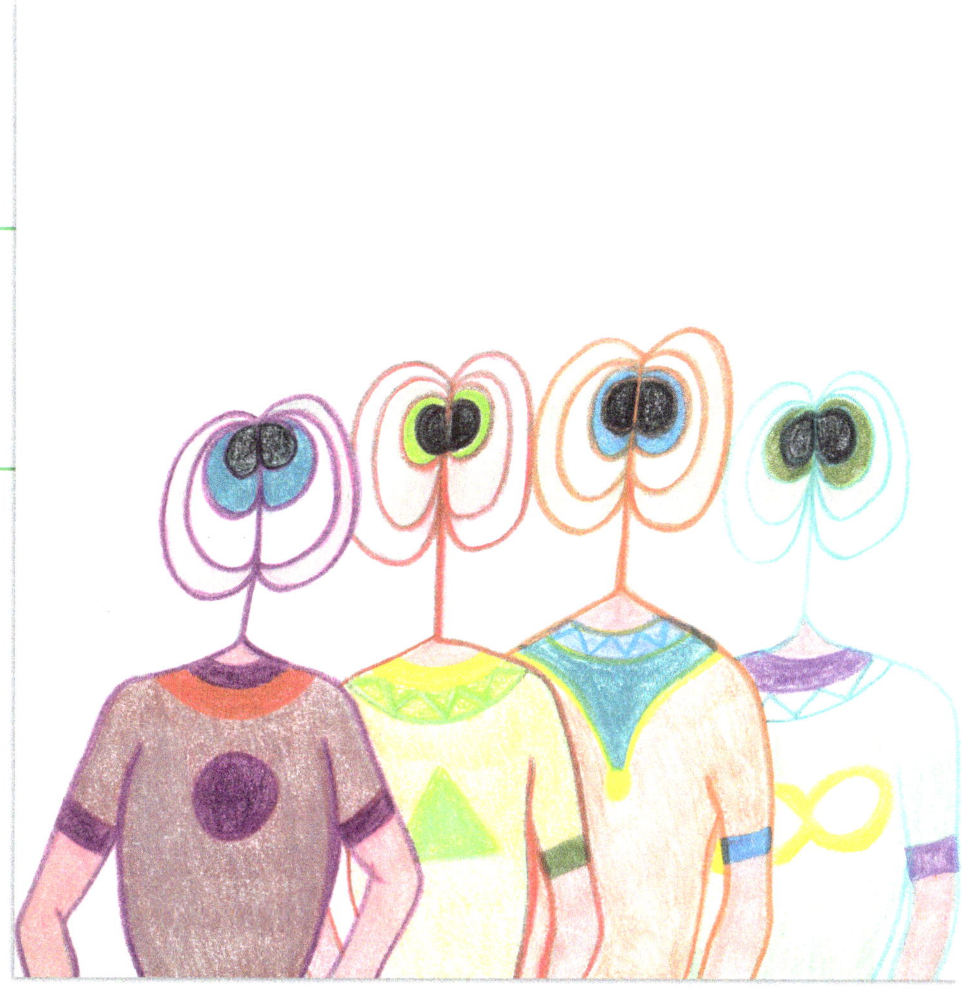

42

WEEK TWELVE

Cultivate Courage

1. Observe your breath for 4 minutes for 7 days. Photograph yourself after.
2. Practice a song for 20 minutes. Sing out the window. LOUD.
3. Before your day begins dance naked. Yes indeed! Naked!
4. What are you tolerating? Why? Do you want it to continue? Why?
5. Learn to say hello in 3 new languages. Use these new words today.
6. Who do you admire? Emulate one of their strongest qualities today. Go.
7. Tell the truth all day. Yikes!

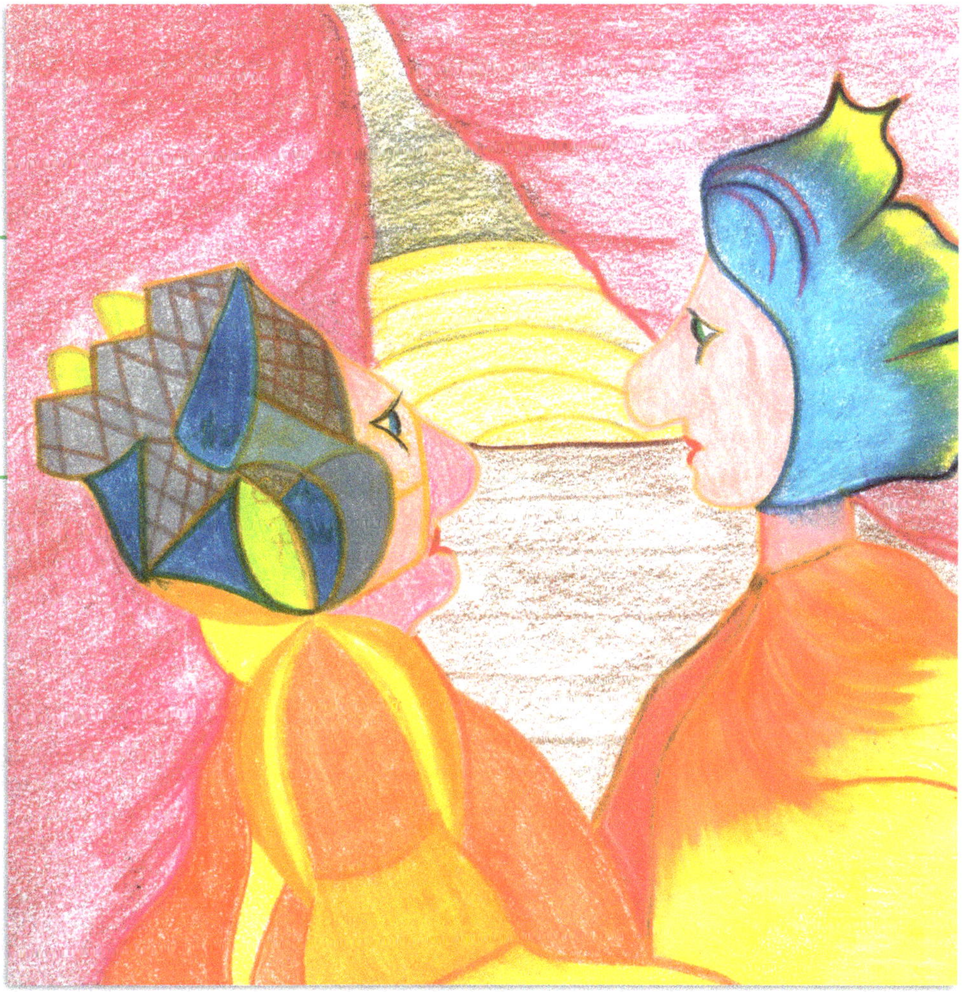

Rest

1. Observe your breath for 4 minutes for 7 days. Lie down after the session.
2. Rest for 20 minutes today. Be silent. Let your body release.
3. Take a solo walk in the majesty of nature. What can you feel and hear?
4. Read for pleasure.
5. Fall asleep listening to music that comforts you.
6. Hold hands with yourself for 3 minutes. Be your own protector.
7. The present moment is your home. Arrive and celebrate being right here.

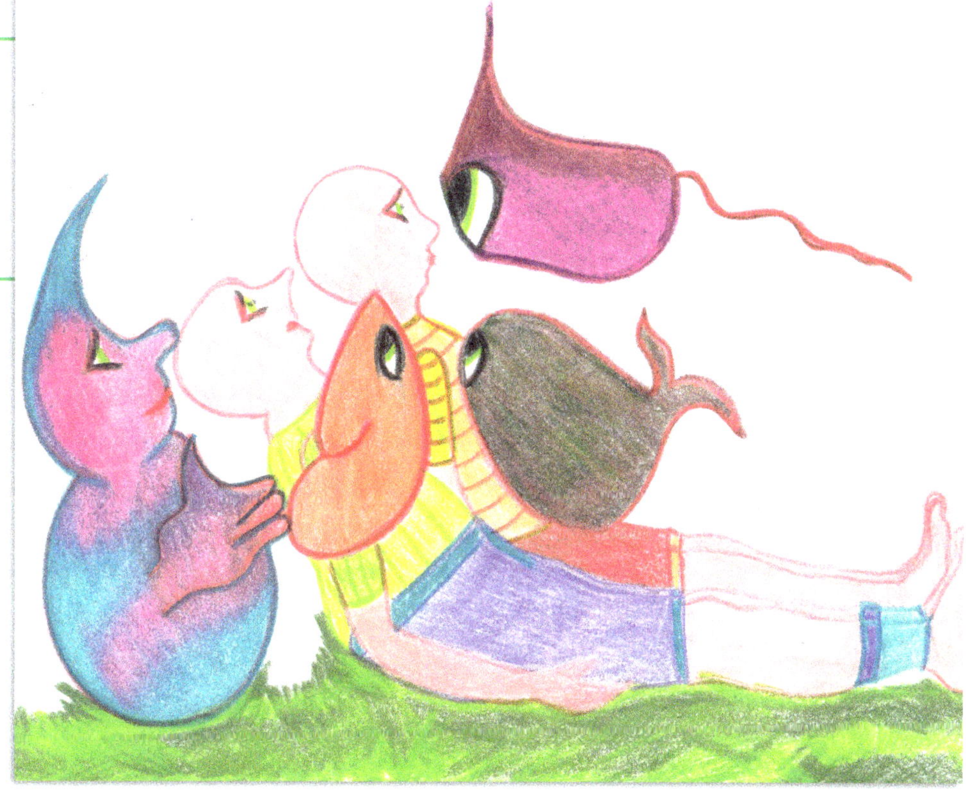

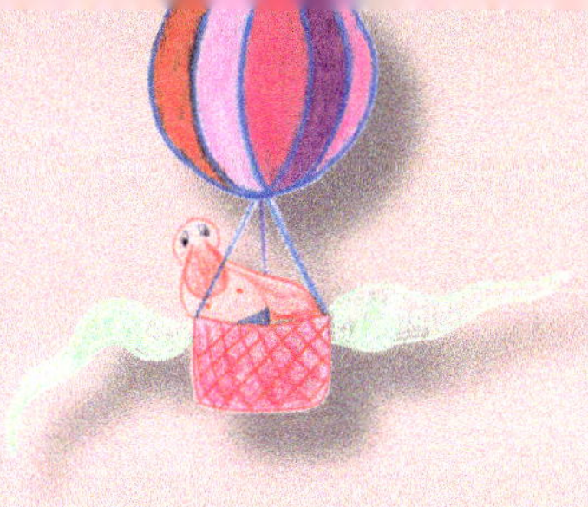

PART TWO

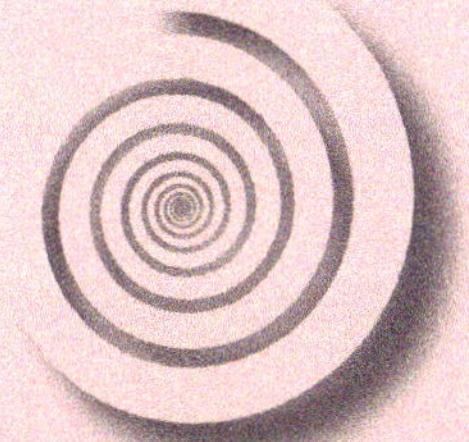

Pay Attention

1. Observe your breath for 4 minutes for 7 days. Rest for 3 minutes post session.

2. Read your poem created Week 11 #7. Now draw an image inspired by your poem.

3. What is the best question you could ask right now? Ask it.

4. Take a different route today. What did you uncover?

5. Look at your face in the mirror. Discover something new. Journal.

6. Uncover a new word in the dictionary. Use it three times today.

7. Do one task at a time. Encounter reverence for what you are doing.

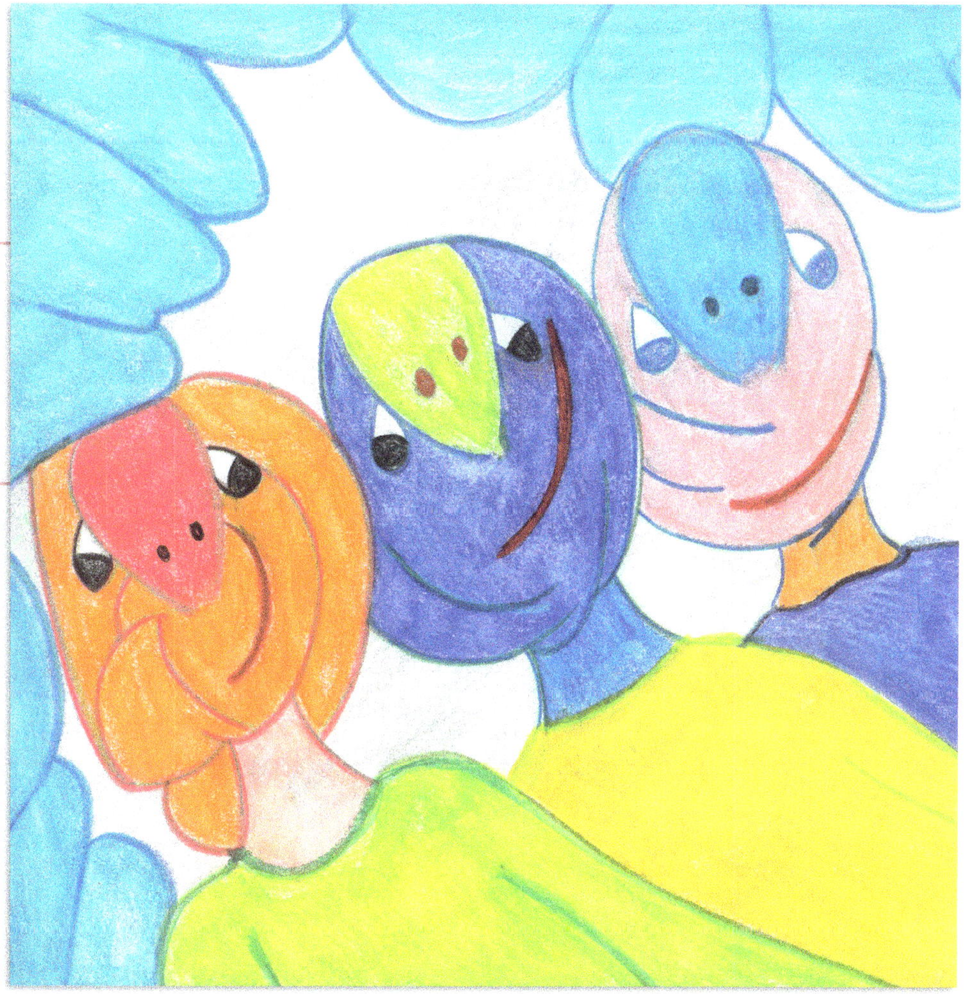

Be Silent

1. Observe your breath for 4 minutes for 7 days. Journal thoughts post session.

2. Observe 20 minutes of silence today. Don't do anything. Just be silent.

3. Stop. Take 10 minutes. Observe the environment. What is present right now?

4. Do you feel alone in silence? Is that okay for you? If not why not?

5. Penetrate a dilemma from a new direction. YOU have the luxury of changing your mind.

6. Walk WITHOUT headphones. Move in sync with your surroundings.

7. Kindness defines character. Are you offering kind language to yourself?

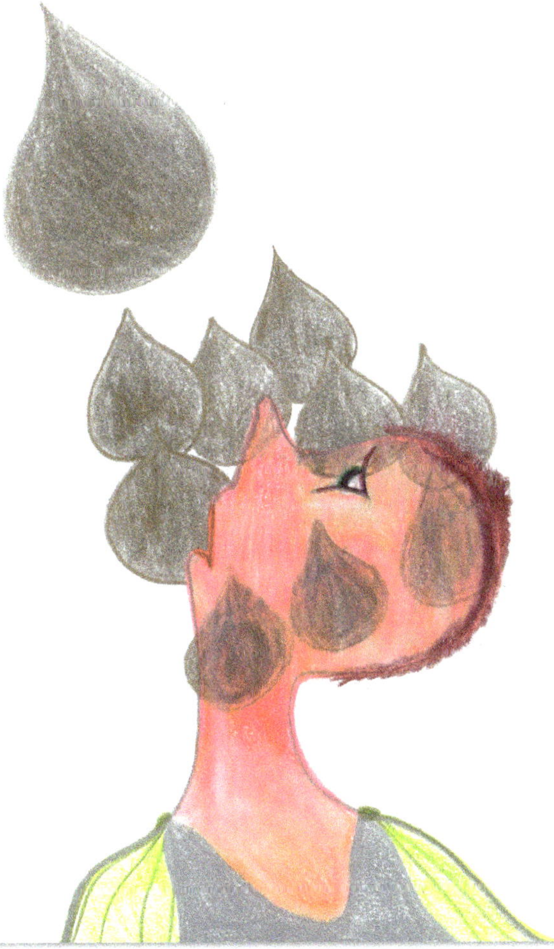

WEEK SIXTEEN

Imagine

1. Observe your breath for 1 minute for 7 days. Do you miss the extra time?

2. Visit a library or bookstore. View book designs that appeal to your aesthetic.

3. Draw 3 things that you love. Cut out your drawings.

4. Begin a new collage using your images from #3. Incorporate design discoveries from #2.

5. Write a love poem to yourself in colour. Cut it up. Add to your budding collage.

6. Draw your feet. Draw your hands. Add to collage.

7. Write a short story, 200 words maximum. Decorate. Add to collage.

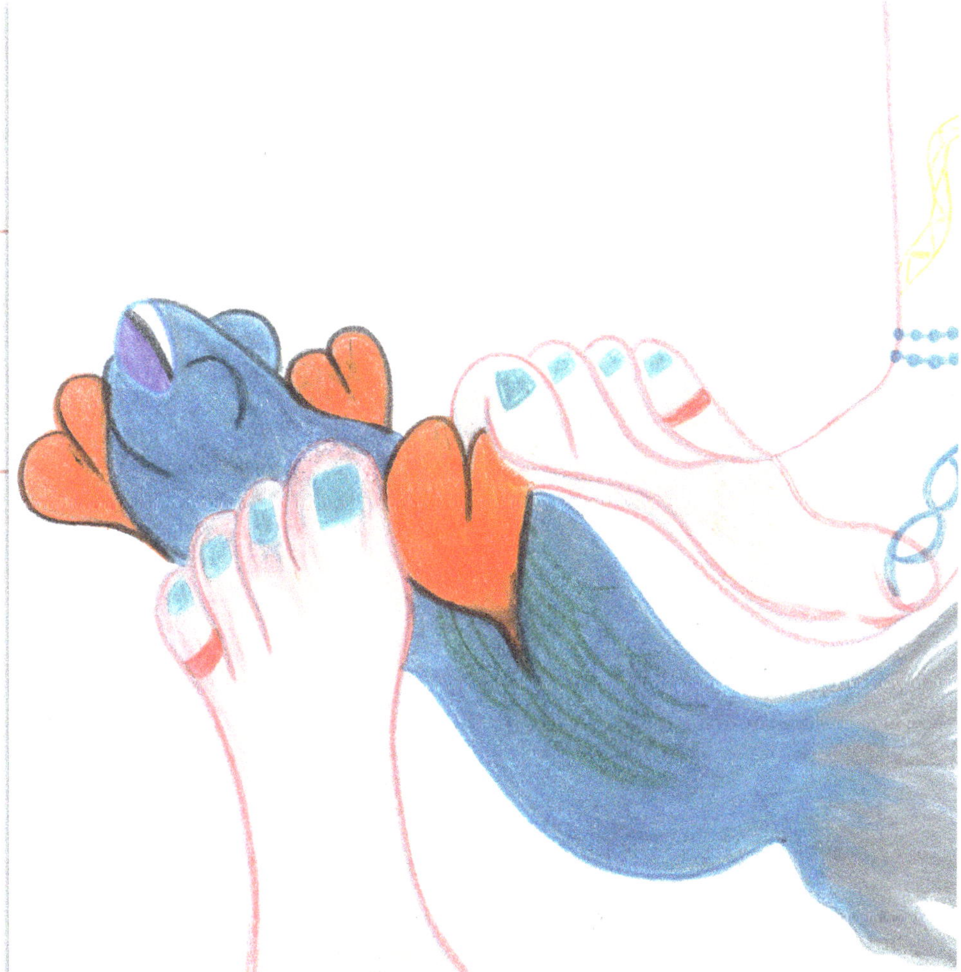

Embrace Mystery

1. Observe your breath for 2 minutes for 7 days morning and night.
2. Visit a garden. Observe a flowering plant. Why does it flower? Research.
3. What exists in black holes? Journal.
4. Think of a loved one. Why do you love them? List impressions.
5. Where do ideas live before they arrive? Visit this place today. Journal.
6. How are you carrying your ancestors? Psychologically? Physically?
7. Where does light come from? Gather information.

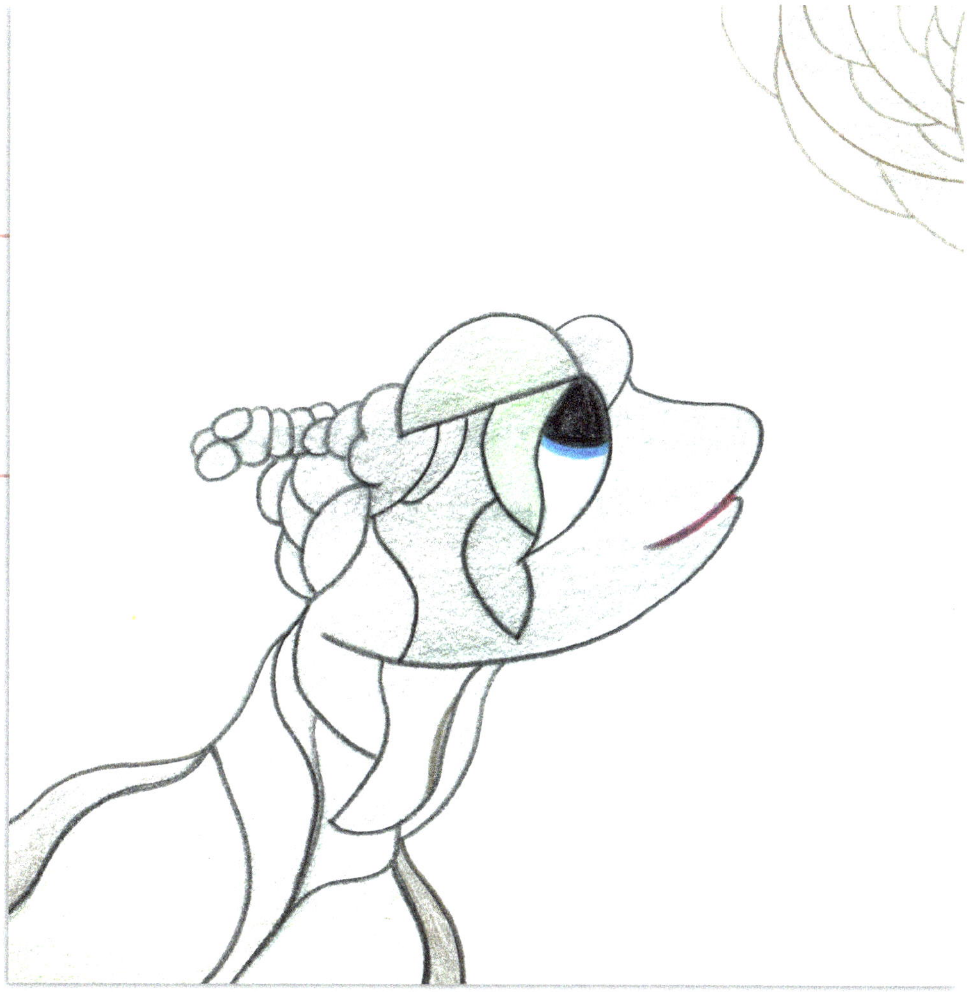

56 WEEK EIGHTEEN

Dream

1. Observe your breath for 3 minutes for 7 days. Blindfolded.

2. Design an ideal day. Make it majestic. Journal ingredients. Begin.

3. Can you dream with your eyes open? What do you see and feel and hear?

4. Listen to new music. Digest the vibrations and the meaning. Allow it to reshape you.

5. Read something inspirational. Any subject. Now take a 10 minute nap.

6. What qualities do you admire? Actively practice them today.

7. Visit a part of your town or city you don't know. Photograph.

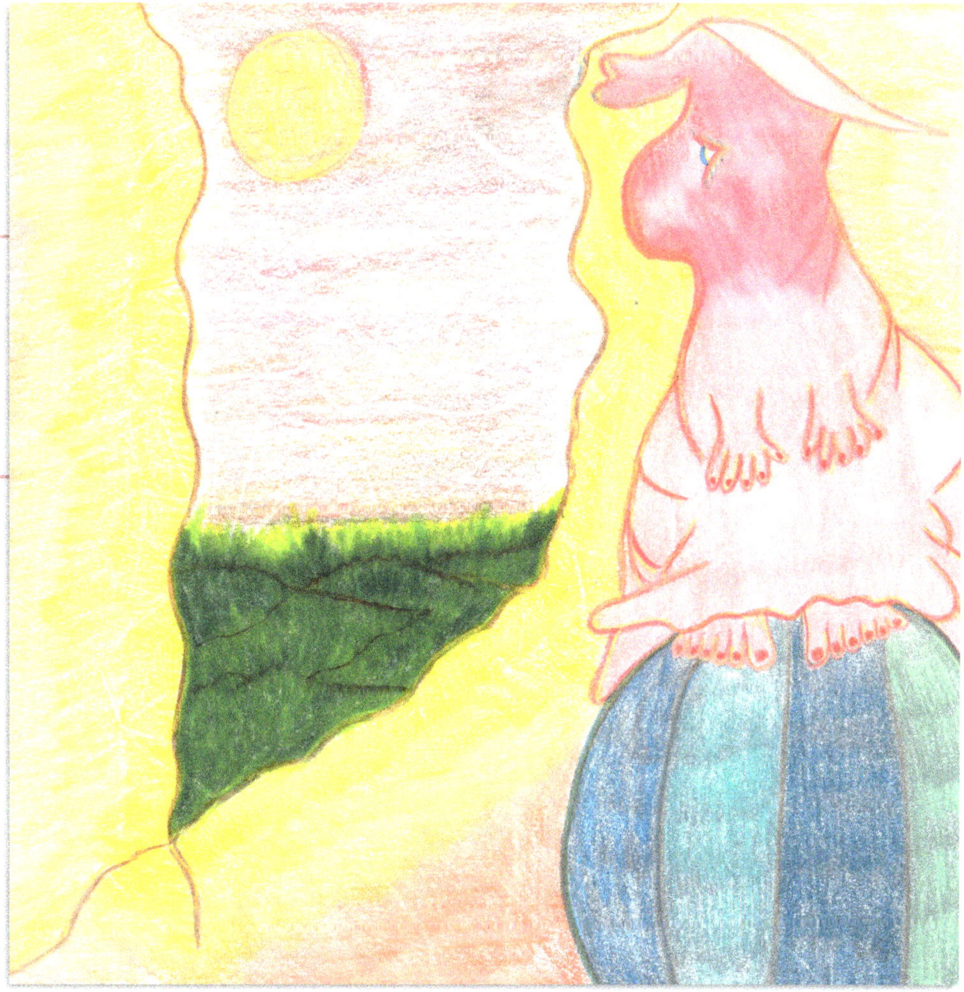

Function

1. List all the habits that help your creativity and all that hinder.
2. Choose a habit that hinders you. Write it a thank you letter. Post it... to anywhere.
3. How do you want to feel today? Cultivate it through action.
4. Recall a recent “mistake.” Celebrate the knowledge gained.
5. Acknowledge one action that you are avoiding. Do it today.
6. When will you be ready? Tomorrow is not guaranteed. Best begin.
7. Empty and tidy one draw in your home. What is taking up space? Why?

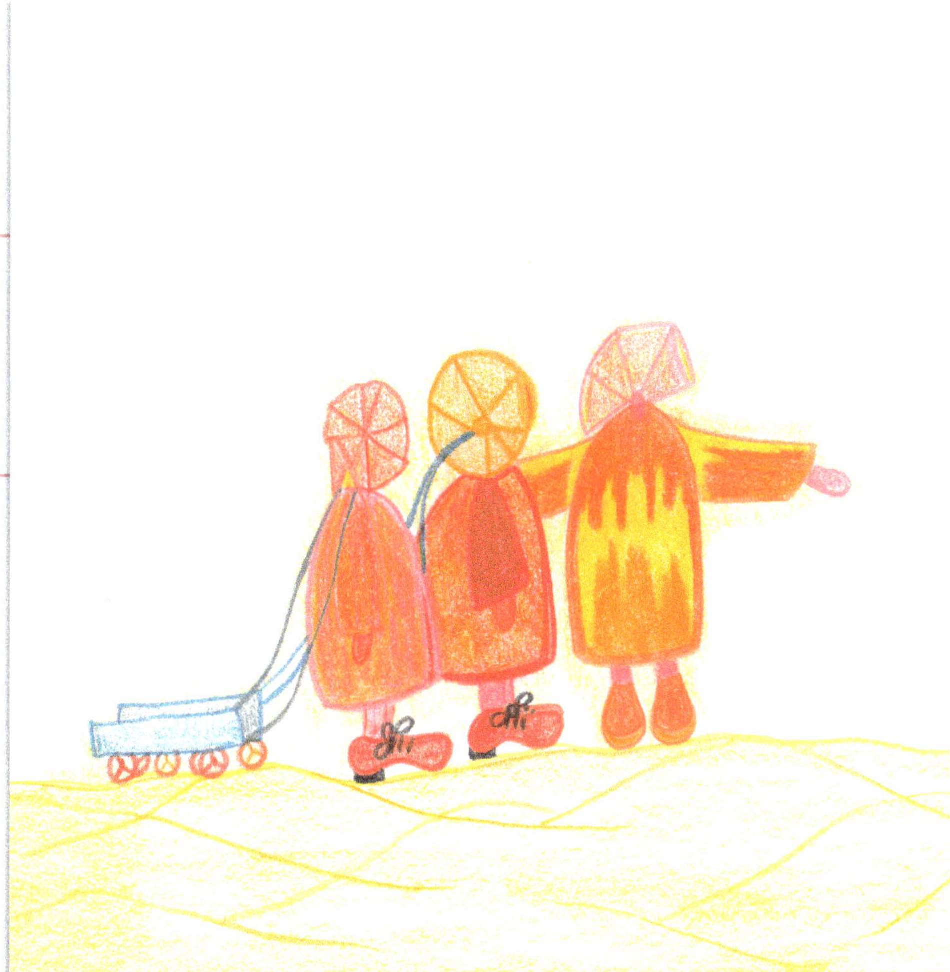

60 WEEK TWENTY

Propagate Presence

1. Observe your breath for 5 minutes for 7 days. Which parts of you are awake? Asleep?

2. Observe your natural breath. Deep? Shallow? Fast? Slow? Now change it for a minute.

3. What aspects of you make you proud? List.

4. How much energy does the task require? Could you be more flamboyant with energy?

5. How does it look to be courageous? List.

6. Draw the qualities of your list from #5. Now action.

7. Take up more space. Allow yourself to expand beyond your skin.

Did you assume that we forgot your breath last week? Did you do it anyway?

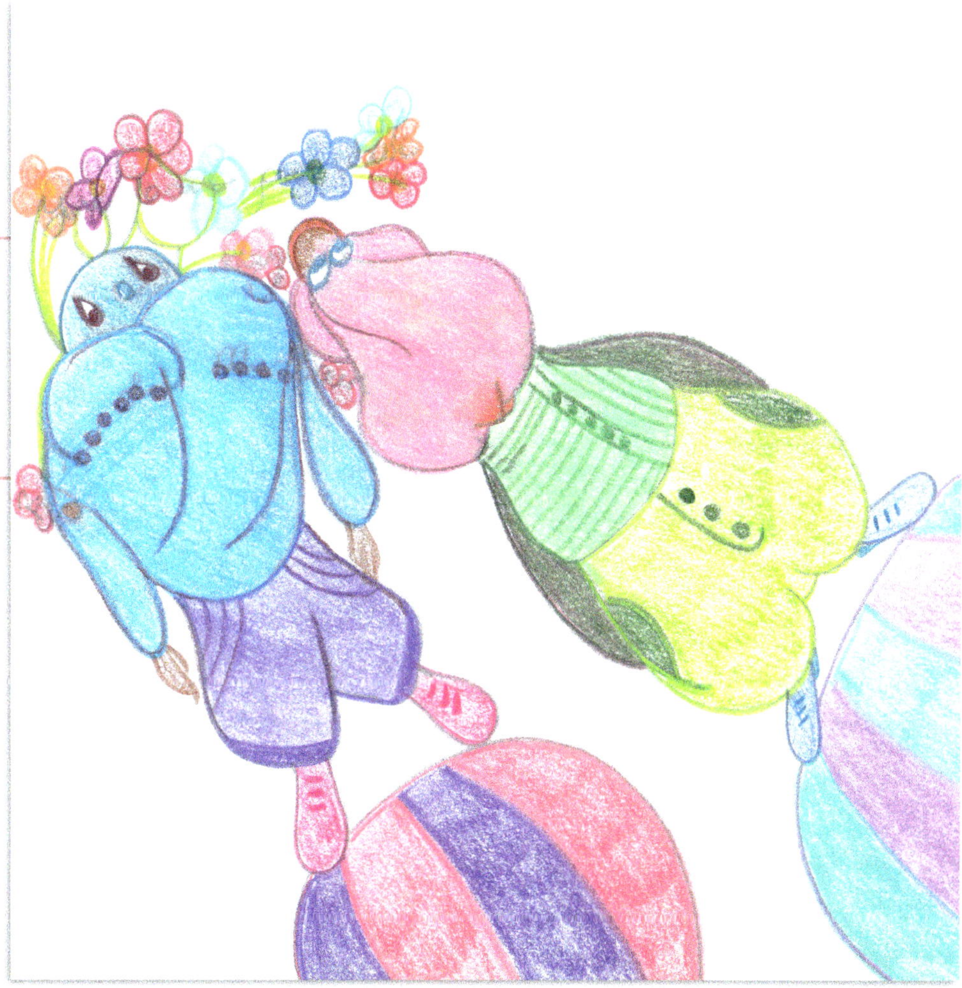

WEEK TWENTY-ONE

Is it?

Revel in Uncert?inty

1. Observe your breath for 5 minutes for 7 days. Acknowledge any dis-ease today.
2. Get your art kit. Choose a theme. Choose a medium. Make art.
3. Challenge it by turning it upside down. This is now the correct way to view it.
4. Admit that you don't know something. Now let out a sigh of relief.
5. Watch a tango video. Try it at home. Record your efforts. Enjoy.
6. Take a photograph of uncertainty.
7. Look at yesterday's uncertainty photo. Journal impressions.

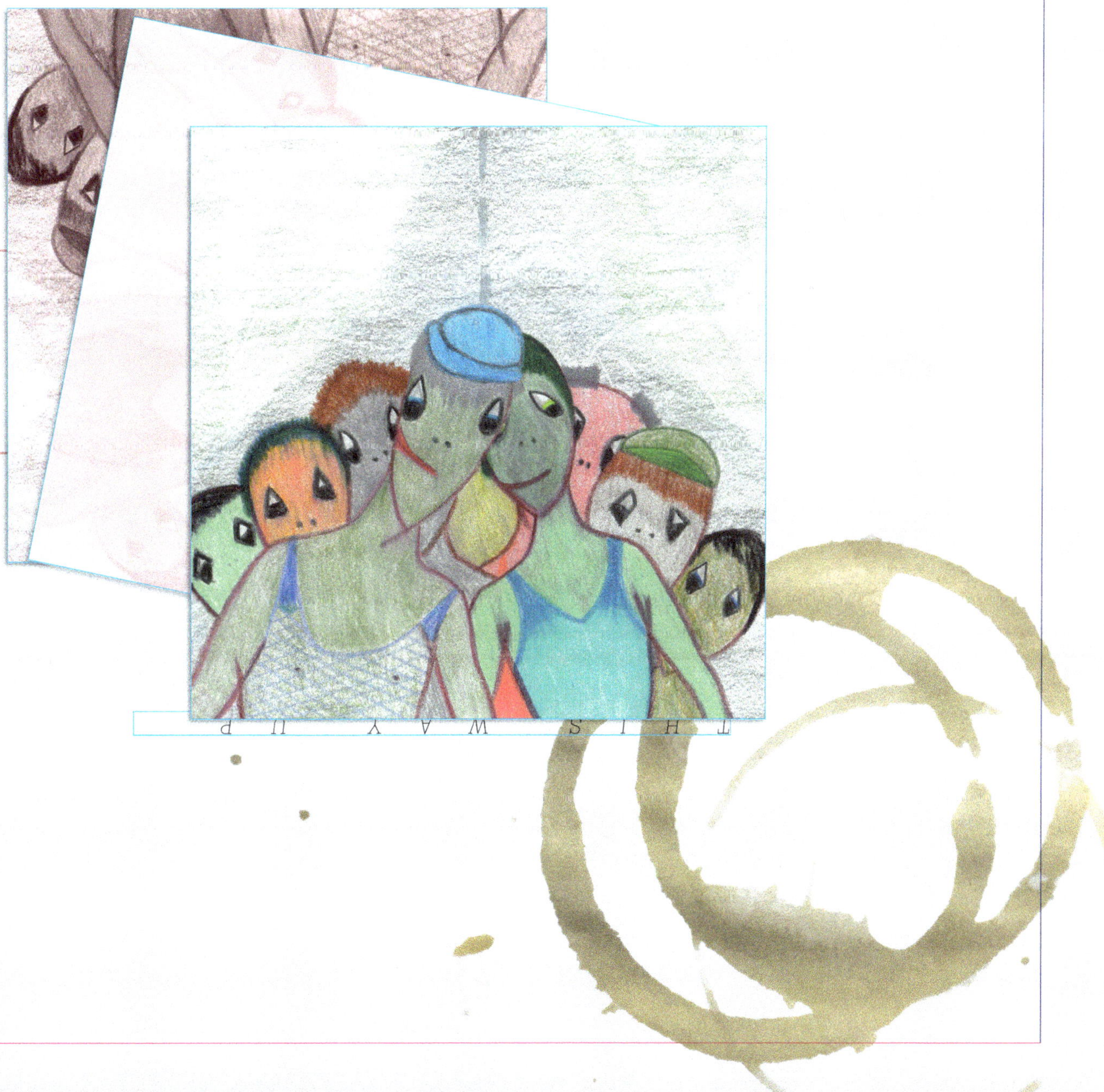
THIS WAY UP

64 WEEK TWENTY-TWO

Generate Patience

1. Observe your breath for 5 minutes for 7 days. Be aware of body sensations. You are ALIVE.

2. Choose a synonym for "Patience." Actively practice it today.

3. Everything of value takes a long time. Are you rushing value?

4. Draw patience. Frame it. Place it by your bed.

5. Do one thing today with precision that advances a goal or dream.

6. Every hour take seven deep inhalations and seven deep exhalations.

7. Look at your schedule. Is it a scaffolding for opportunity and creation?

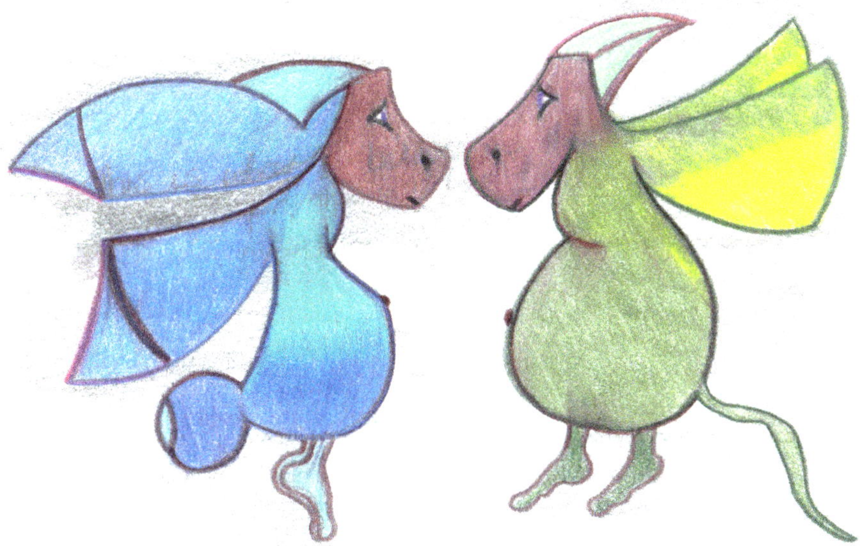

Offer Mercy

1. Observe your breath for 6 minutes for 7 days. Rest for 6 minutes.

2. What do you understand about Love? What do you need to understand?

3. How are you competing with yourself? Ponder and journal.

4. Are you reliable? Yes? How? If not, why not?

5. Choose two seemingly unrelated objects, position them as a still life.

6. What do you discover about the above two objects? Draw results.

7. Embrace the possibility that you could forgive.

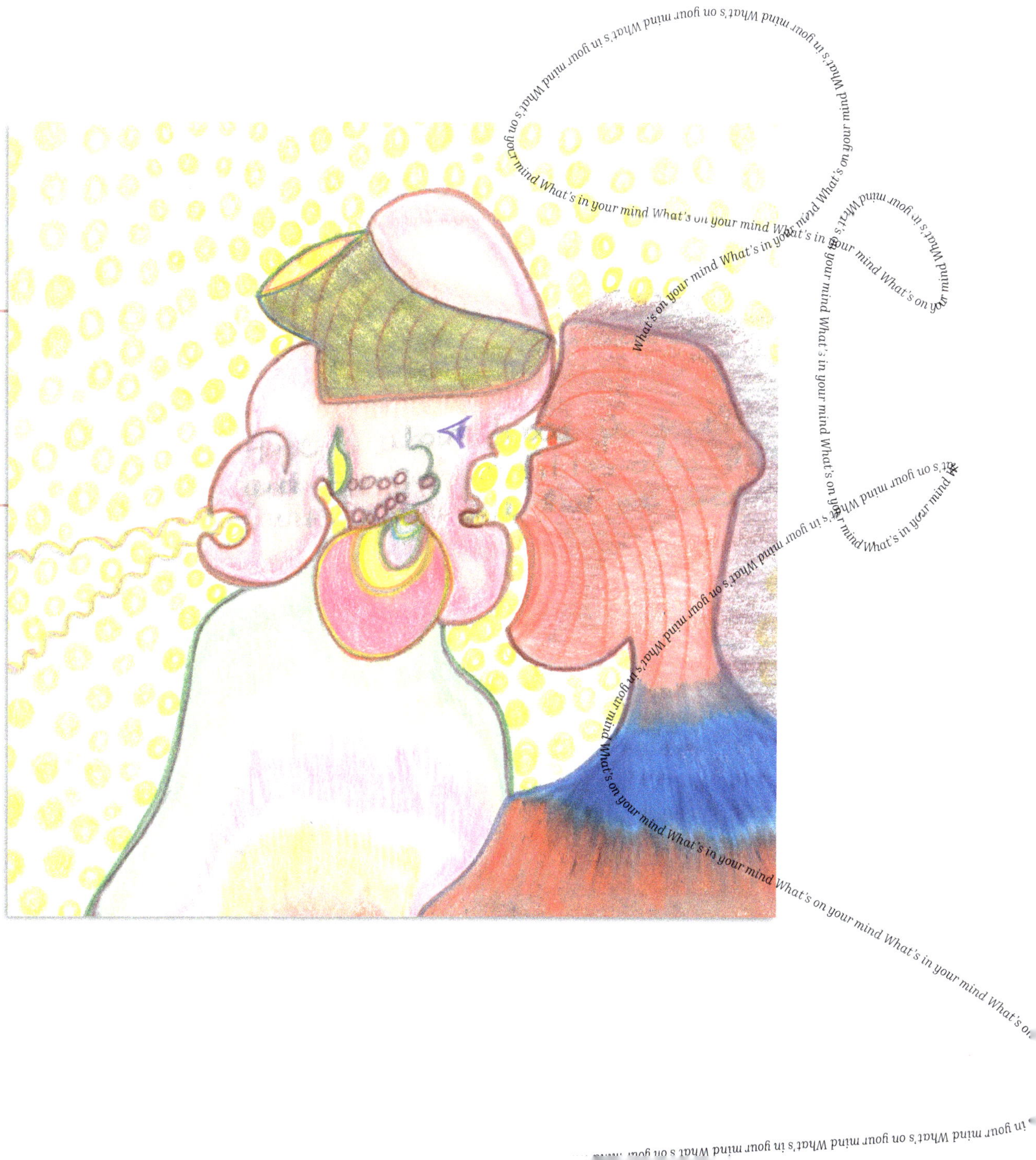
What's on your mind What's in your mind

Rejoice in Wonder

1. Observe your breath for 6 minutes for 7 days. Light a candle, make a wish.
2. Where do clouds go? Journal your findings.
3. Take a magnifying lens and study your skin. What do you see? Amazing huh?
4. Wear a smock. Go make art “en plein air!” Why not?
5. Daydream for 20 minutes. That’s it. Just daydream. You don’t need a reason.
6. When did you last gasp with wonder? Maybe it is time to do that again?
7. Write four joyous possible scenarios for your future life. Pick one. Begin.

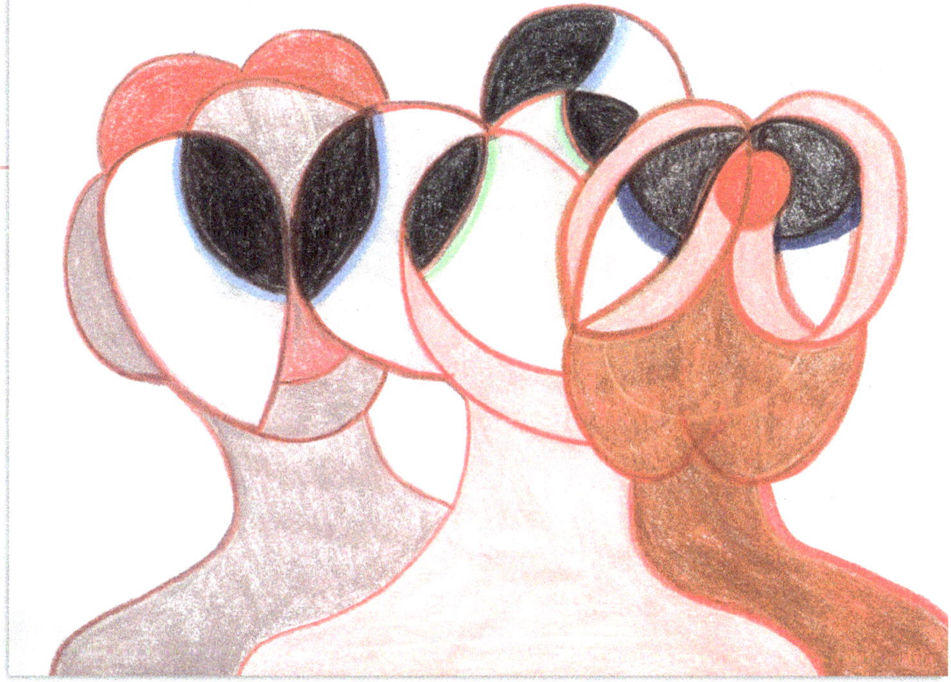

Offer Gratitude

1. Observe your breath for 6 minutes for 7 days. Pause. Be grateful.
2. Let today's mantra be "thank you".
3. Write a letter of gratitude and send it... to yourself. Be generous.
4. Have you ever been helped? Then you know how. Begin.
5. Before eating anything today observe the food and give thanks.
6. What are you taking for granted? Stop.
7. Can you move, see, hear, taste, smell or feel? Lucky, huh?

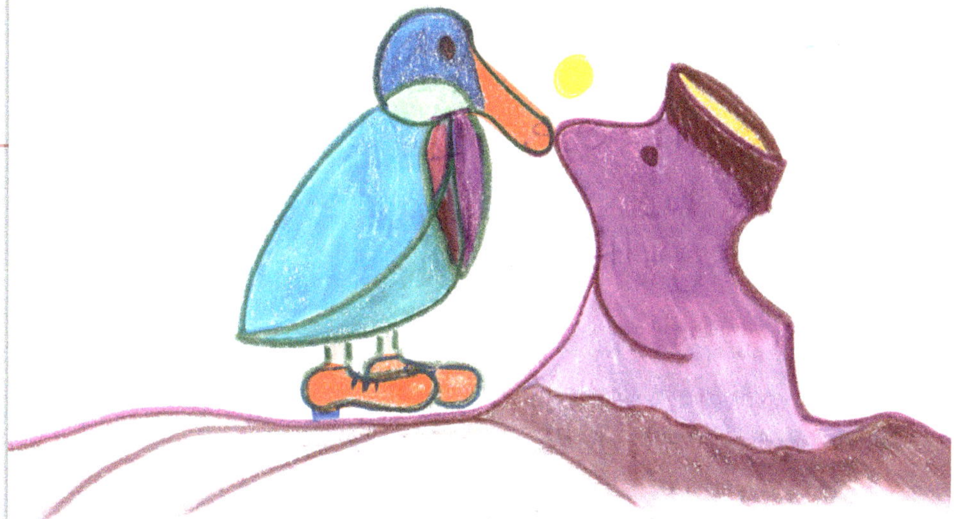

WEEK TWENTY-SIX

Hope

1. Observe your breath for 7 minutes for 7 days. Wash your hands.

2. Admit you don't know, draw hope from your admission. Now take a 10 minute nap.

3. Hope lives here. It is just waiting for you to notice.

4. List 3 people who magnify your spirit. Plan a visit to rejoice in that energy.

5. Play triumphant music, go to a window, call out, "I live in hope."

6. Journal all of your hopeful thoughts. Make it colourful.

7. Who could you collaborate with to make the whole thing easier? Ask.

How does it feel knowing it's already been half a year? Enjoy that feeling...

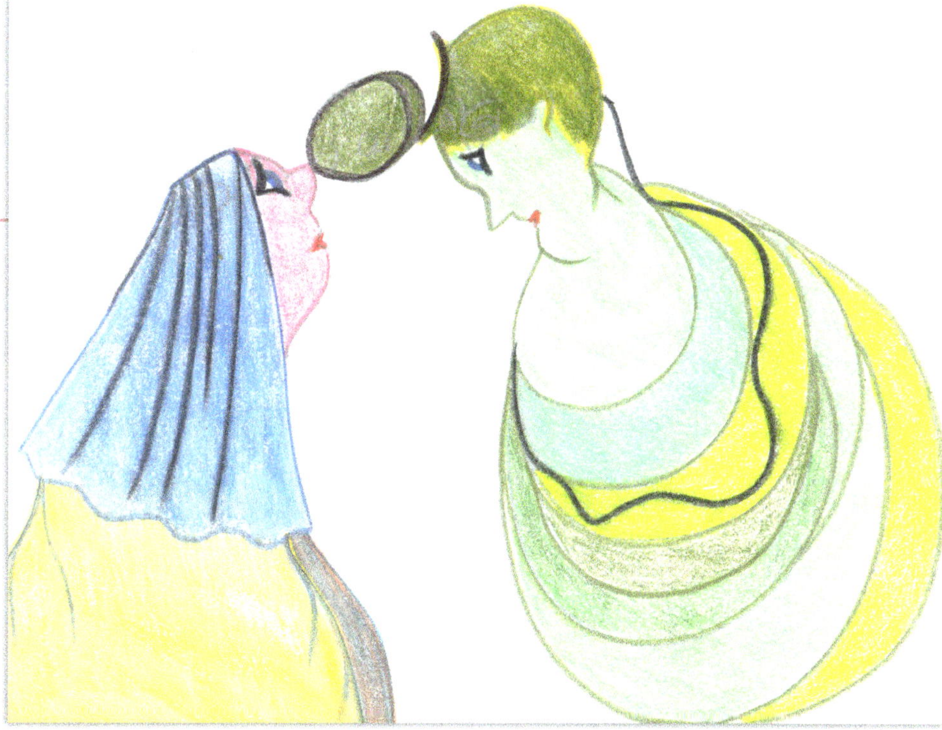

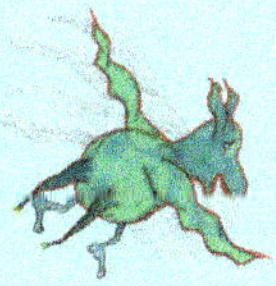

PART THREE

Pay Atenttion

1. Observe your breath every day for a period of your choice for 7 days.

2. View and memorise an image. Write down what you remember. Check results.

3. List 3 things you do regularly. Stop. Observe them with deep devotion today.

4. Record yourself speaking about your day. Listen to the recording. Who is that?

5. Create a list of people who encourage you creatively. Phone one.

6. Go for a 10 minute walk somewhere new. Register impressions.

7. Drink 3 glasses of water before 10am.

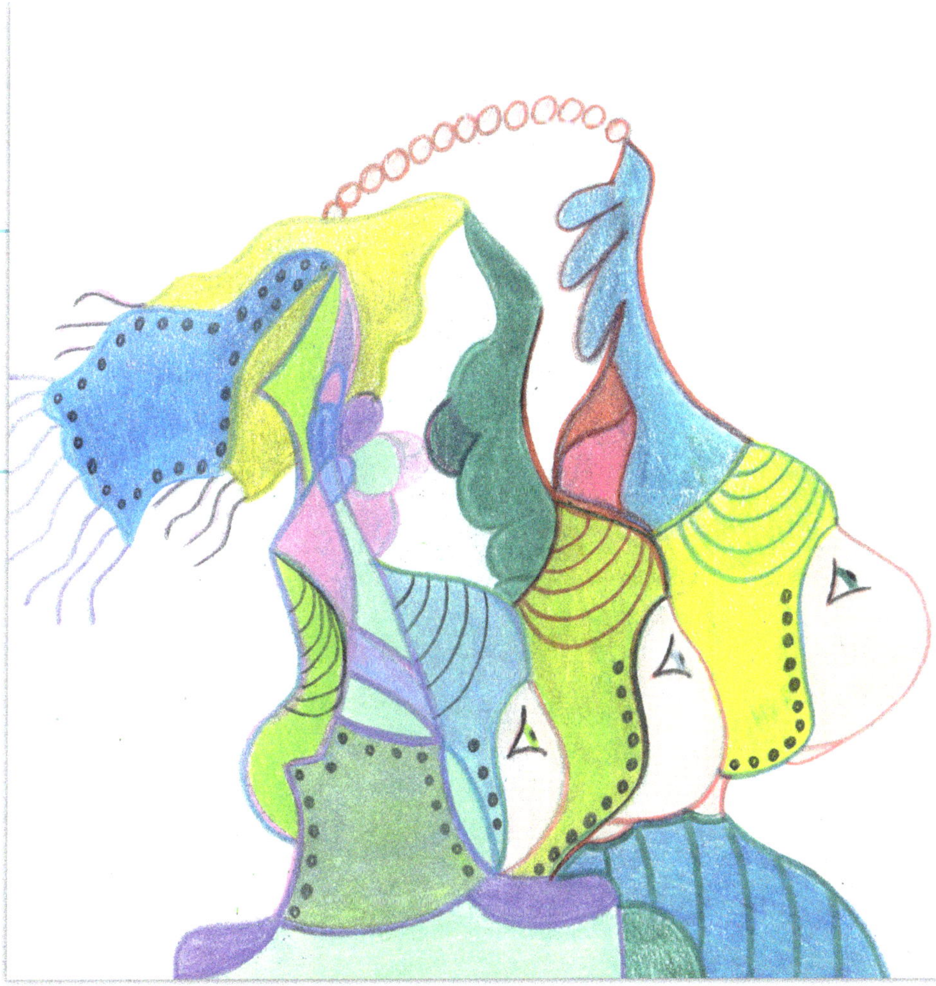

78 WEEK TWENTY-EIGHT

Surrender

1. Observe your breath for 8 minutes for 7 days. Make a wish for another.

2. Take a nap for 10 minutes each day. Raise your legs if possible.

3. Make amends today and mean it. Don't include the word BUT or IF.

4. What aren't you managing? Ask for help.

5. Listen to orchestral music of your choice. Listen all the way to the end.*

6. There is no shortcut. Practice is the answer. Put some skin in the game.

7. Look up. Look down. Look outside. Look inside. Now decide.

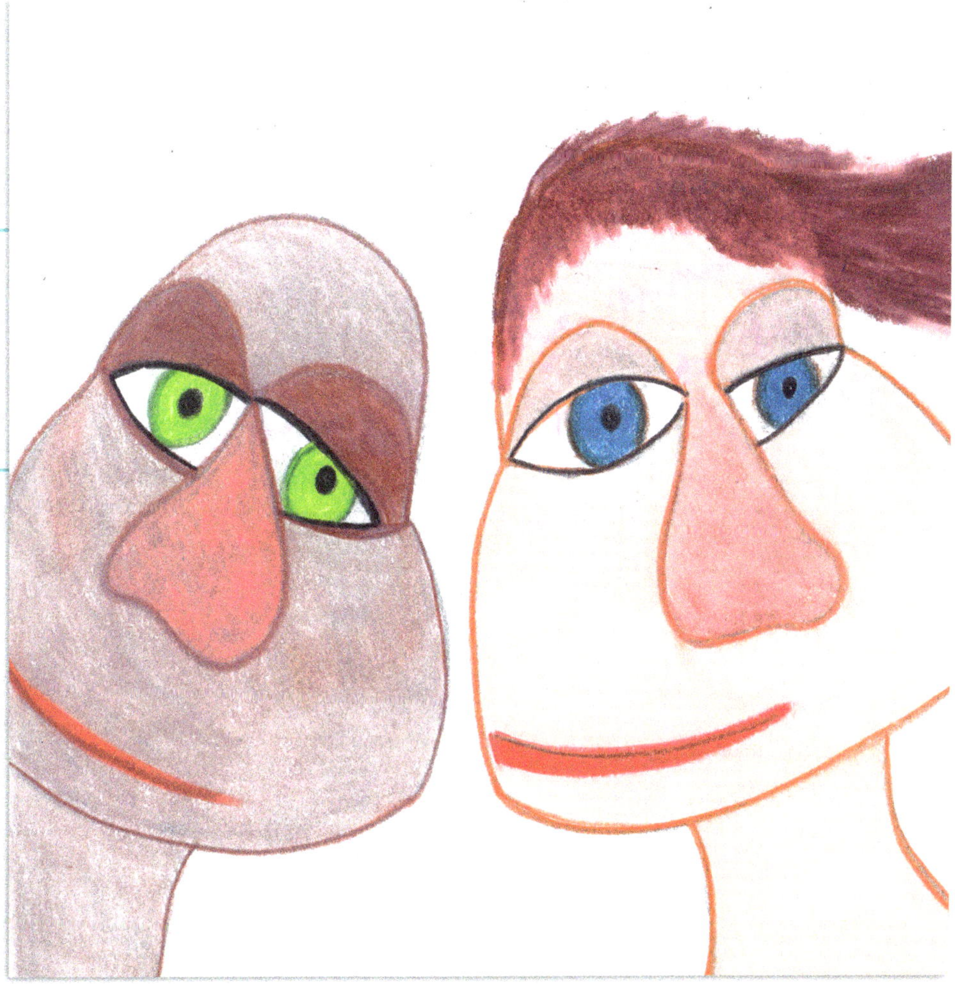

80 WEEK TWENTY-NINE

Honour

1. Observe your breath for 8 minutes for 7 days. What needs resolution?

2. Do you lie? Why? Stop today.

3. What are you most afraid of? What would you like to do about it?

4. What is the one decision could you make to help yourself? Do it today.

5. Research an act of GREAT HUMANITY. Incorporate realisations today.

6. What door have you closed? Is that what you want?

7. Begin a week free of all intoxicants. Don't wait - start right now.

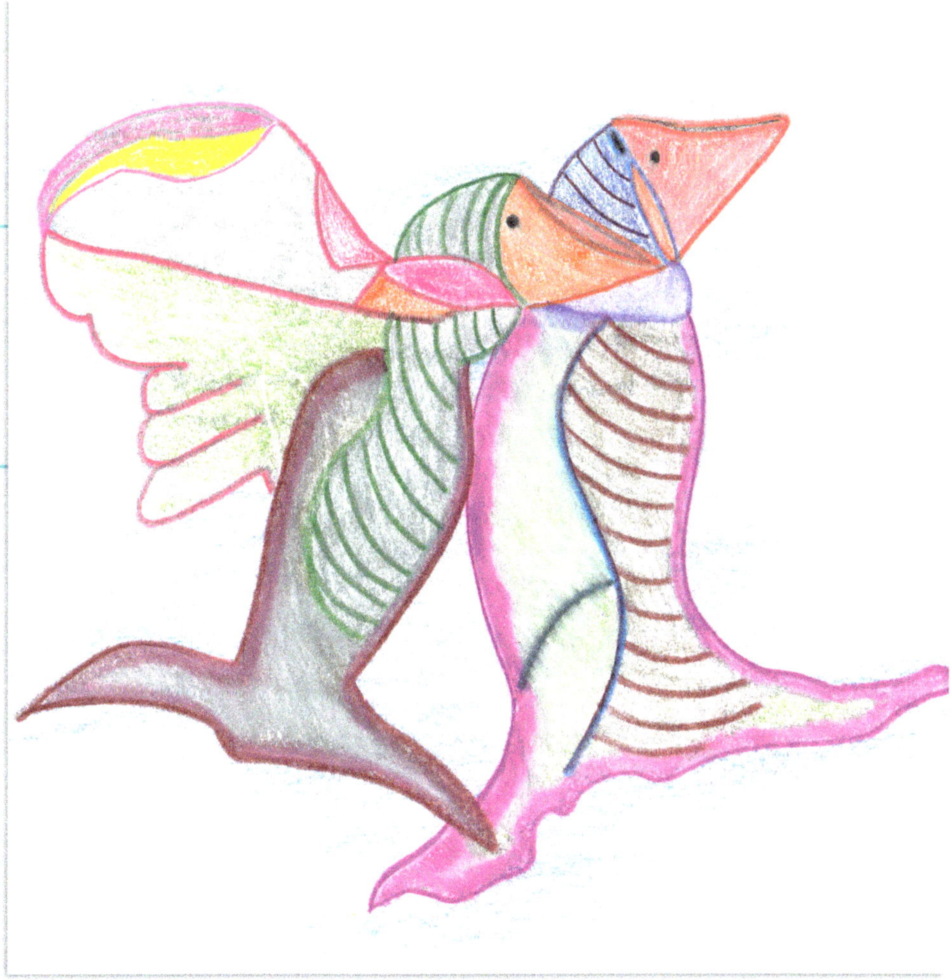

Give

1. Observe your breath for 7 minutes for 7 days. Then read inspiring material. *

2. Write a letter of encouragement to another person. Send.

3. Gift something of value to a stranger. Think outside the box.

4. Offer YOURSELF your full attention for 20 minutes. What do you need?

5. Slow down. Sit down. Give grace. Offer hope to another in any form.

6. Donate... time, love, money, hope, forgiveness, opportunity. Do it.

7. Make a totem to generosity with materials in your environment. Gift it to another.

Did you manage 7 days without intoxicants? If not, why not?

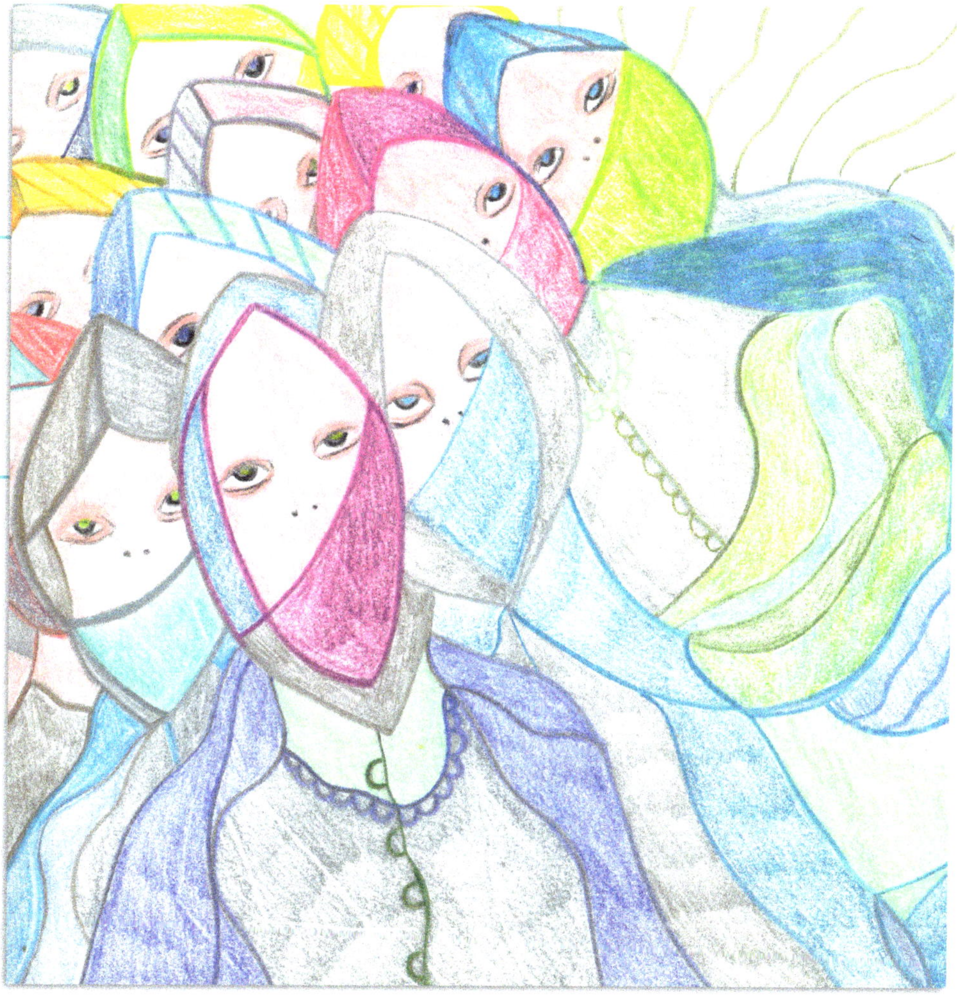

Respect

1. Observe your breath for 8 minutes for 7 days. Morning and night.
2. How do you want to be treated? Do that for others.
3. Eat smaller portions this week. Record what you eat when and why?
4. Exercise for 20 minutes. Is this normal? Make it so.
5. Extend your sleep time. Give yourself the rest you need.
6. What is your relationship to discipline? Order can be your greatest ally.
7. Have you given to your community lately? Action a giving plan.

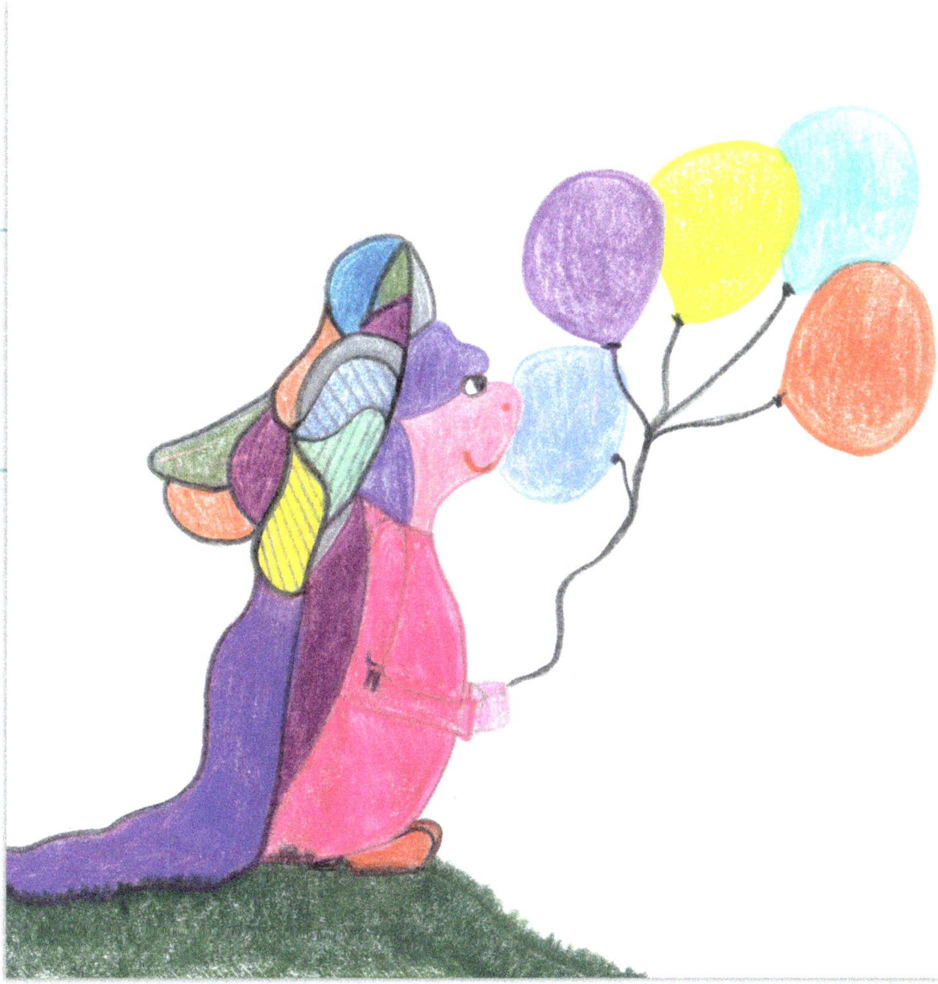

Accept

1. Observe your breath for 8 minutes for 7 days. What qualities would you like to foster in yourself?

2. Take inspired action on regrets today. How best can you repair this?

3. What knowledge do you need to achieve an aim? Access help as needed.

4. If it is not true don't say it.

5. If it is not right don't do it.

6. Your time is precious. Are you squandering it? Schedule wisely.

7. Accept your own terror. Yes, terror. It will help you to accept it in others.

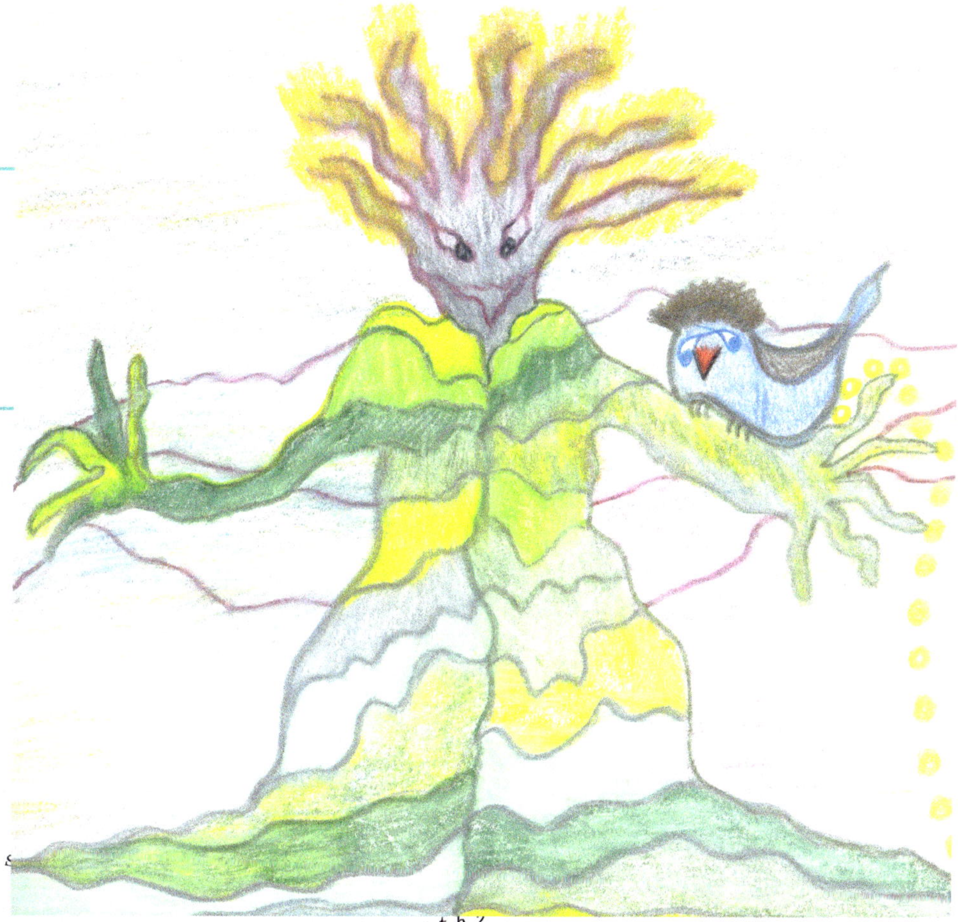

what's

underneath?

Co-operate

1. Observe your breath for 9 minutes for 7 days. Journal experience.
2. Avoid noise today. Encourage quiet contemplation. Pay attention to your responses.
3. Allow your thoughts to curve today. Consciously soften your grip. Ahhh.
4. What 2 things can you connect to create an unexpected outcome?
5. Daydream for 20 minutes. No result required.
6. What do you wish someone would ask you to do? Well, do it.
7. Begin so someone else can follow. Flourishing is mutual.

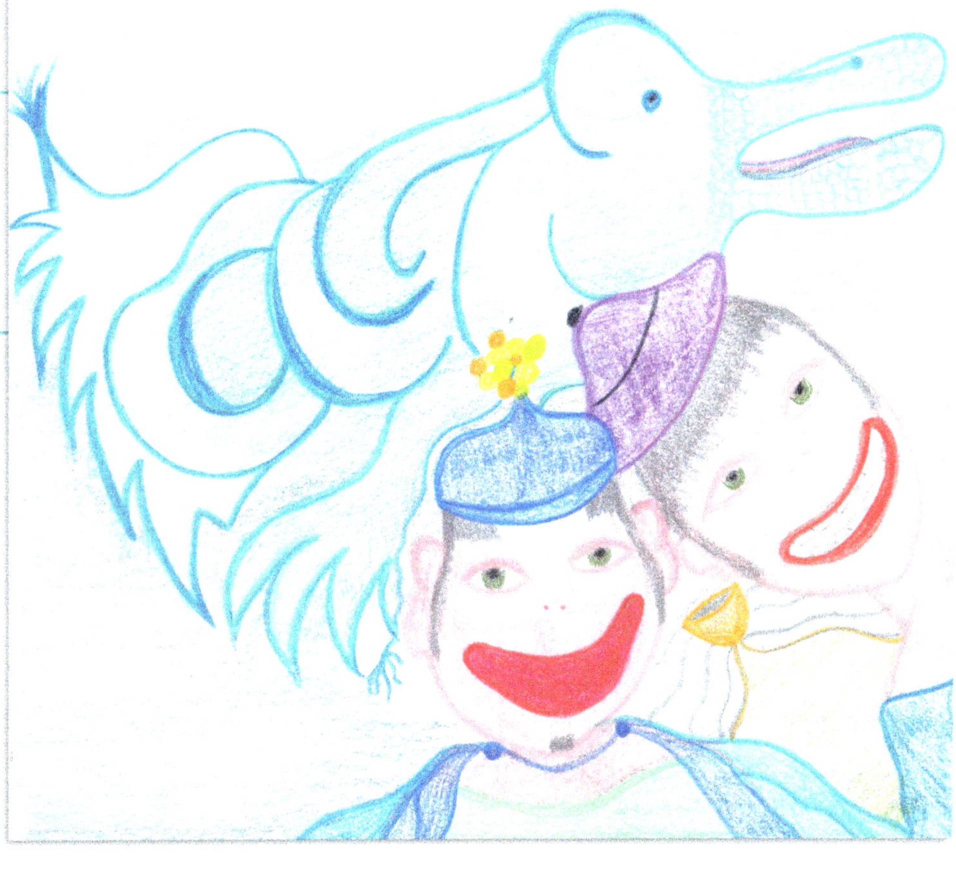

Apologise

1. Observe your breath for 9 minutes for 7 days. What would you like to confess today?

2. Find 6 synonyms for the word apology. What resonates with you? Embody this today.

3. Where is your limit and why did you put it there? You can re/move it.

4. Are you at moral ease? If not why not?

5. Write a wholehearted apology... to yourself. Be clear and concise.

6. What do you understand about yourself that you didn't before the apology?

7. If today was a chapter in a book, what would it be called?

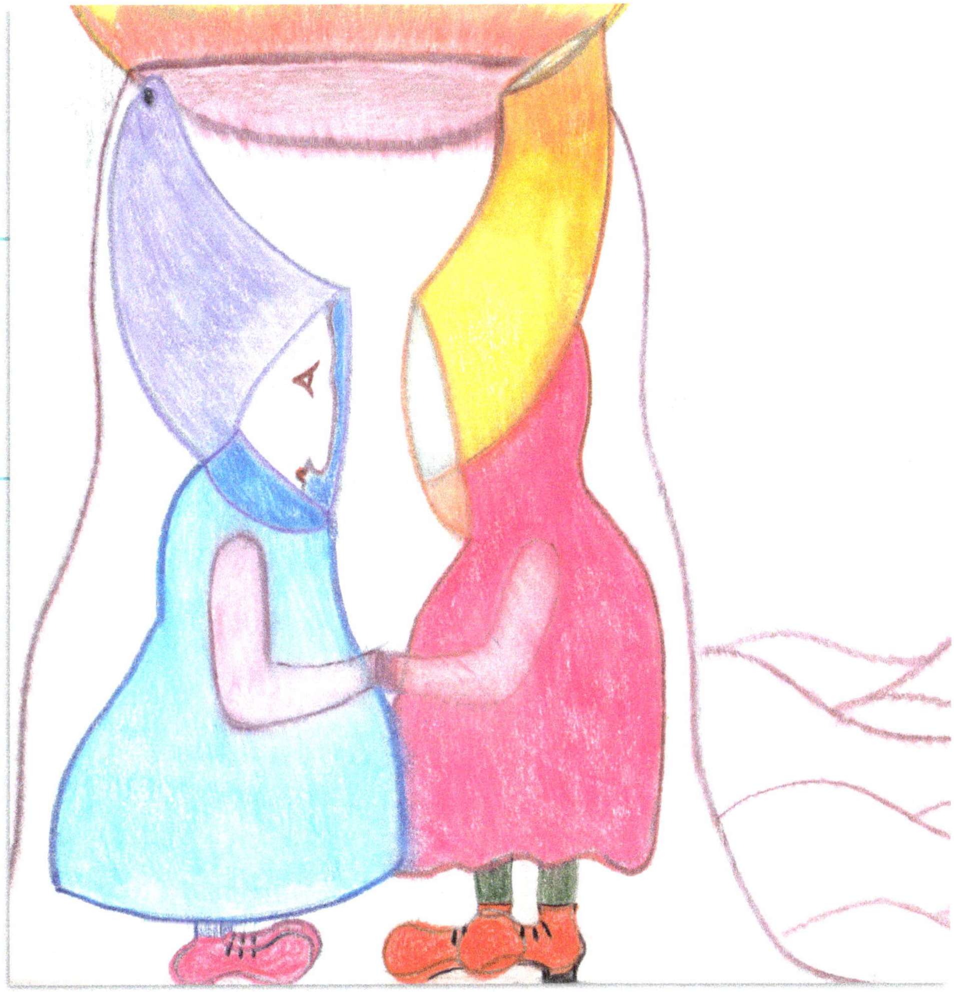

Magnify Intimacy

1. Observe your breath for 1 minute for 7 days. Do you miss more time?
2. Take a walk in nature. Be awed by your existence. Communicate with your surroundings through observation.
3. What don't you know about yourself? You are infinite. Ask questions.
4. Ask a loved one what they need in order to flourish. Then give it.
5. What do you cherish? Tell someone. Tell yourself. Tell the world.
6. When did you last really pay attention to what they are saying?
7. Cultivate one thing today that will promote WISDOM. Not intellect. WISDOM.

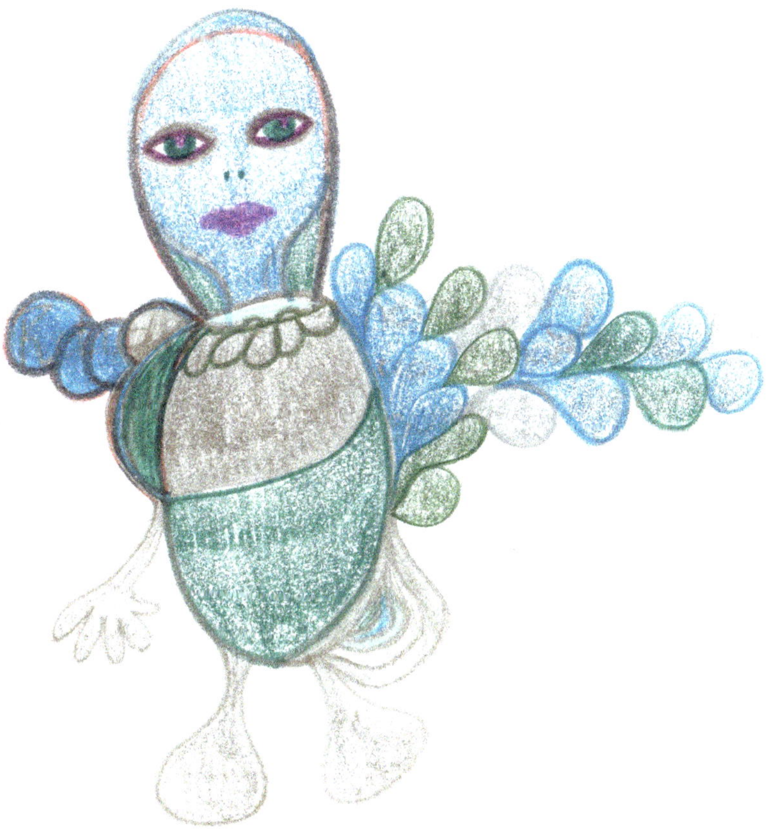

Cultivate Ritual

1. Observe your breath for 9 minutes for 7 days. Two sessions in nature.

2. Cultivate a morning ritual that calms and inspires you.

3. Let language nourish you. Form a great sentence. Be enriched by words. Journal.

4. Plan ahead, make a special day... for YOU. Set a date with you.

5. Open the windows. Clean the bathroom. Honour the space to honour yourself.

6. Stop. Surrender to the passing of time. Let go. Let life unravel.

7. Work methodically on a problem regardless of how long it takes.

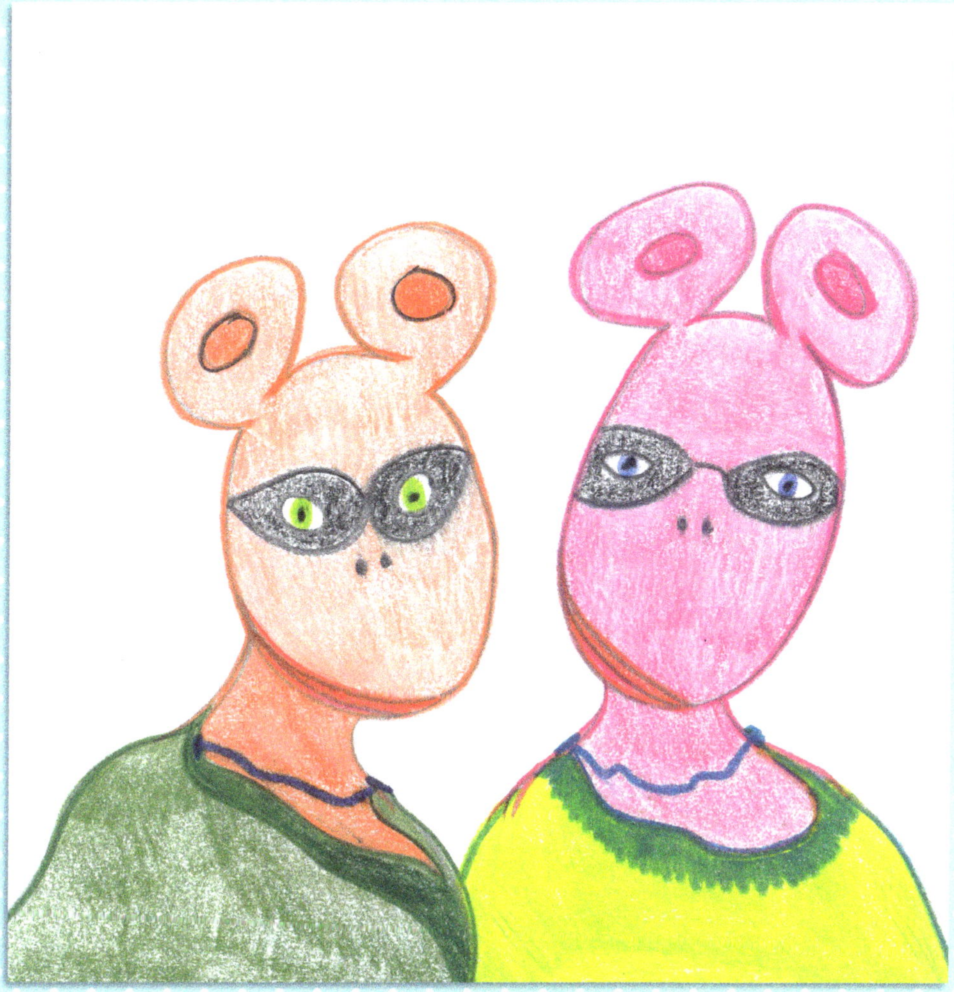

Bring to Fruition

1. Observe your breath for 10 minutes for 7 days. Everything is changing, even you...
2. Take six photos this week that express Fruition.
3. Search for a painting from another time that expresses Fruition for you.
4. Draw your image of Fruition. Pin it up. Contemplate the image.
5. List your accomplishments. Place up where you can see.
6. Create a self portrait.
7. Using all your images from this week create a 'Fruition Collage'.

Good morning! How's Week 36 #2 going?

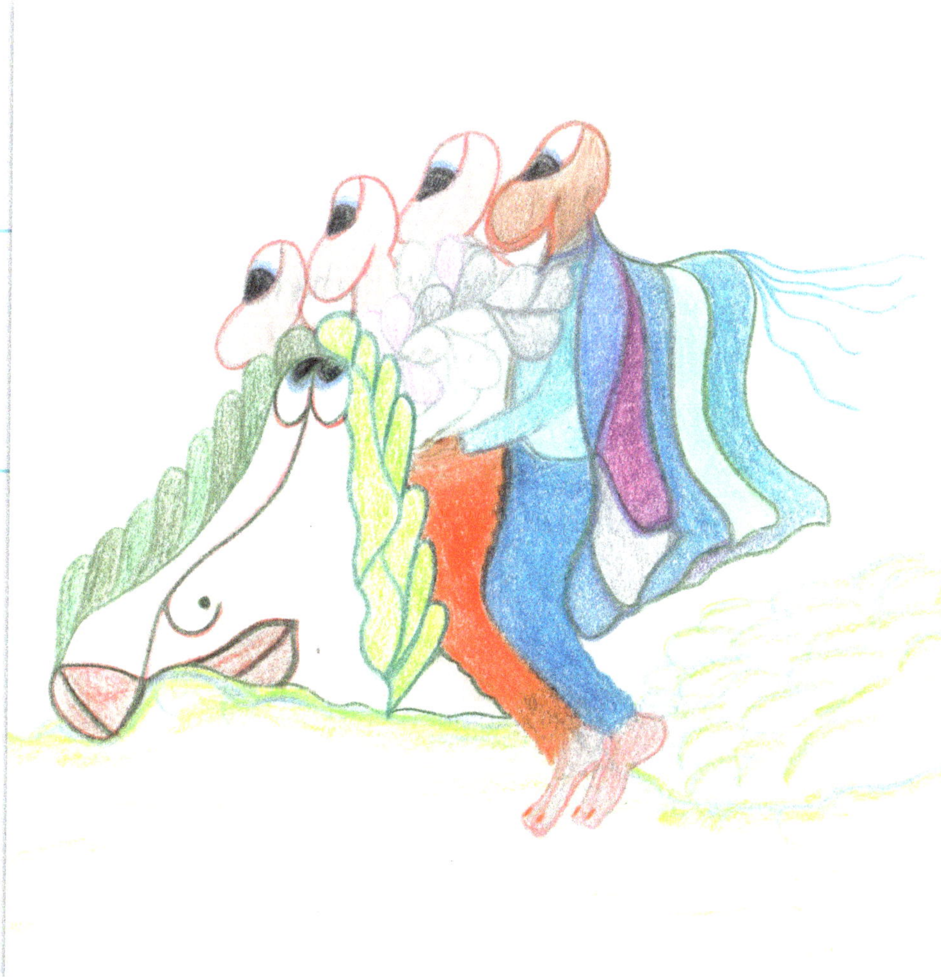

98 WEEK THIRTY-EIGHT

Love

1. Observe your breath for 6 minutes for 7 days. Astonishing isn't it.

2. Nurture someone with your full attention each day this week.

3. How many cells does your body have? There is so much to love.

4. Do you know what you are talking about? If not be quiet.

5. What do you enjoy? Have you paid it any attention lately?

6. Listen intently. Don't interrupt. Be patient. Then ask questions.

7. Can you be genuinely excited by the success of others? Generosity is potent.

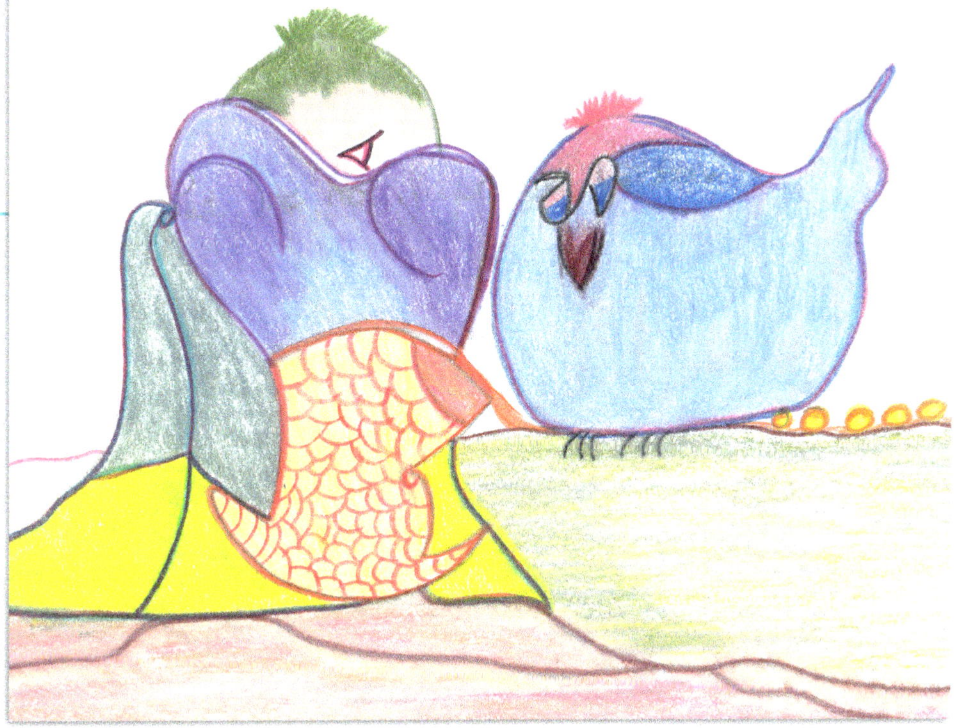

Discover Peace

1. Observe your breath for 1 minute for 7 days. Rest for 9 minutes for 7 days.
2. Nap as often as you want for the rest of the week.
3. Go without TV for the remainder of the week. Read/draw/rest/write/listen to music. Dream.
4. Go out and get lost somewhere. Welcome the new with open arms.
5. How do you receive? Gifts arrive in many forms. Might you be more welcoming?
6. Draw a peace symbol. Photograph and keep it on your phone to remind you.
7. What is Proud Flesh in reference to a horse? How might you apply it?*

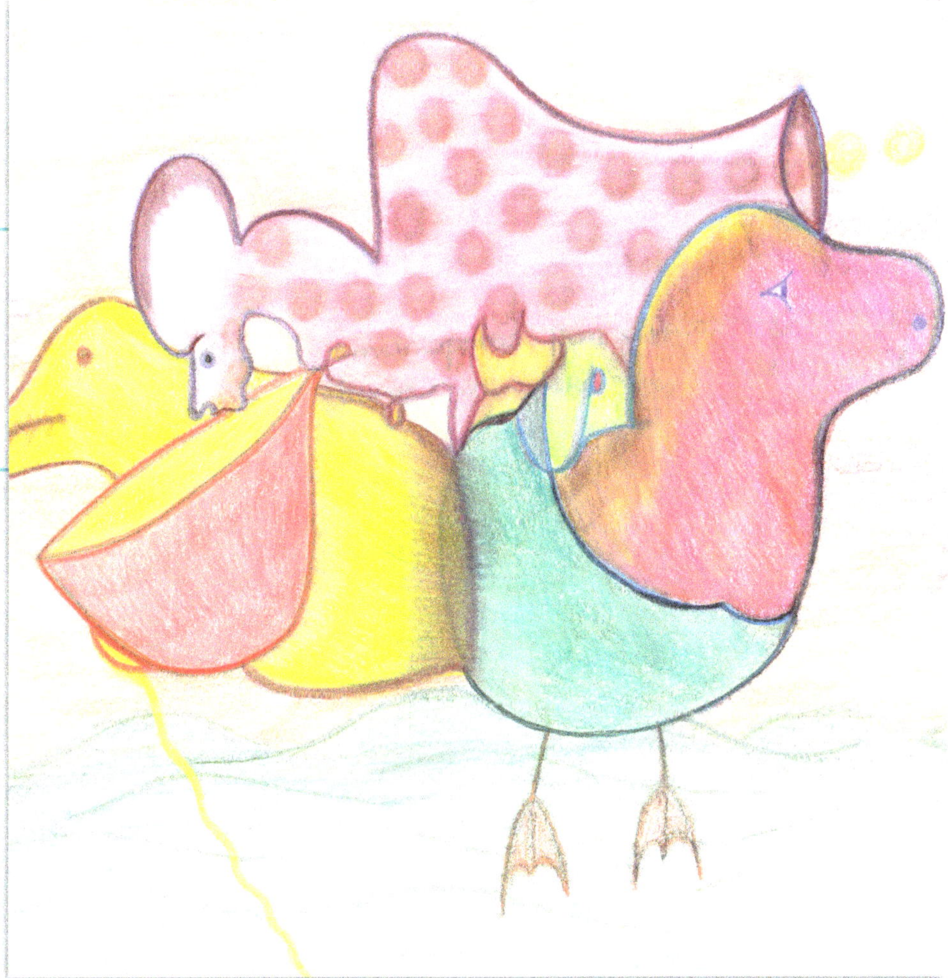

PART F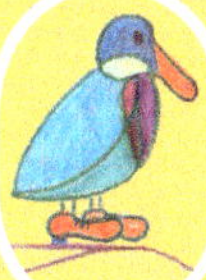UR

Pay Attention

1. Observe your breath for 6 minutes for 7 days. Drink a herbal tea.
2. Mail a postcard to yourself. Choose the image carefully.
3. Look for the colour Silver today. Photograph results. Did you find any?
4. Every hour for 30 seconds listen to yourself breath.
5. Slow dance to music you love. Move in new ways.
6. Write everything in pen today.
7. Listen to a new music for 5 minutes today...or more.*

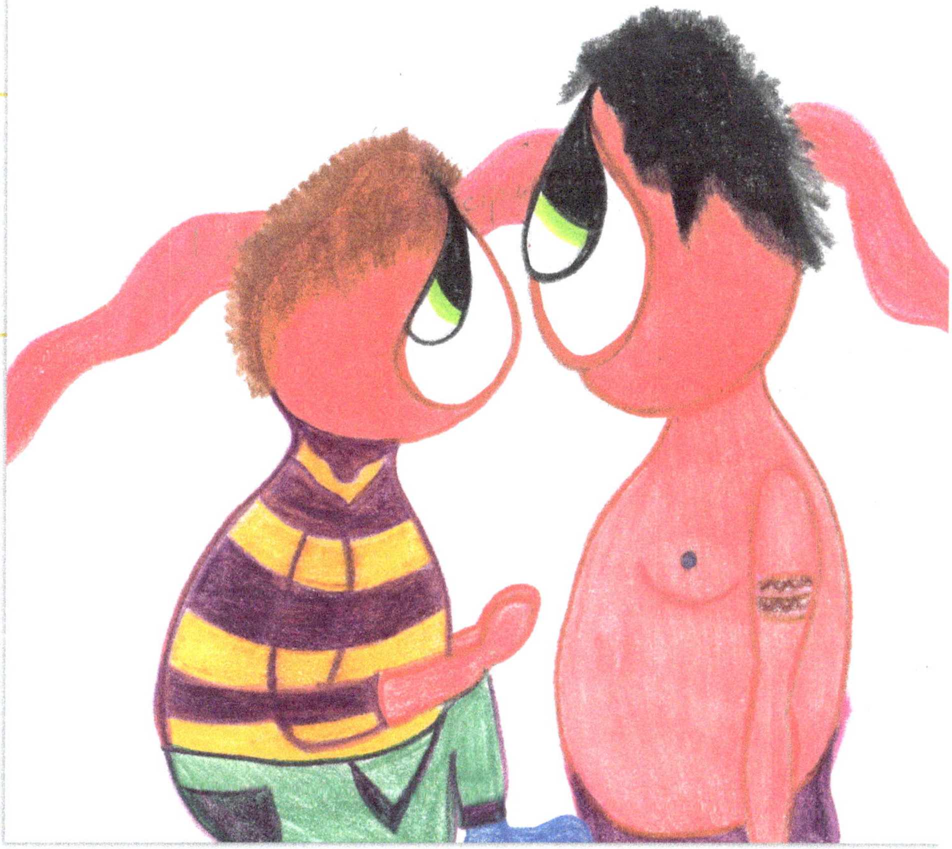

WEEK FORTY-ONE

Uncover Your Nature

1. Observe your breath for 10 minutes for 7 days. Journal for 10 minutes.
2. Sincerity is shown in action. What is your current action?
3. How could you provide encouragement today... to you.
4. Endurance counts for a lot. How could you cultivate more if needed?
5. Swap clothes with a friend. Experience a new style.
6. Ask a loved one to write you a list of all your great qualities. Frame.
7. You are your most important project. Are you your own priority?

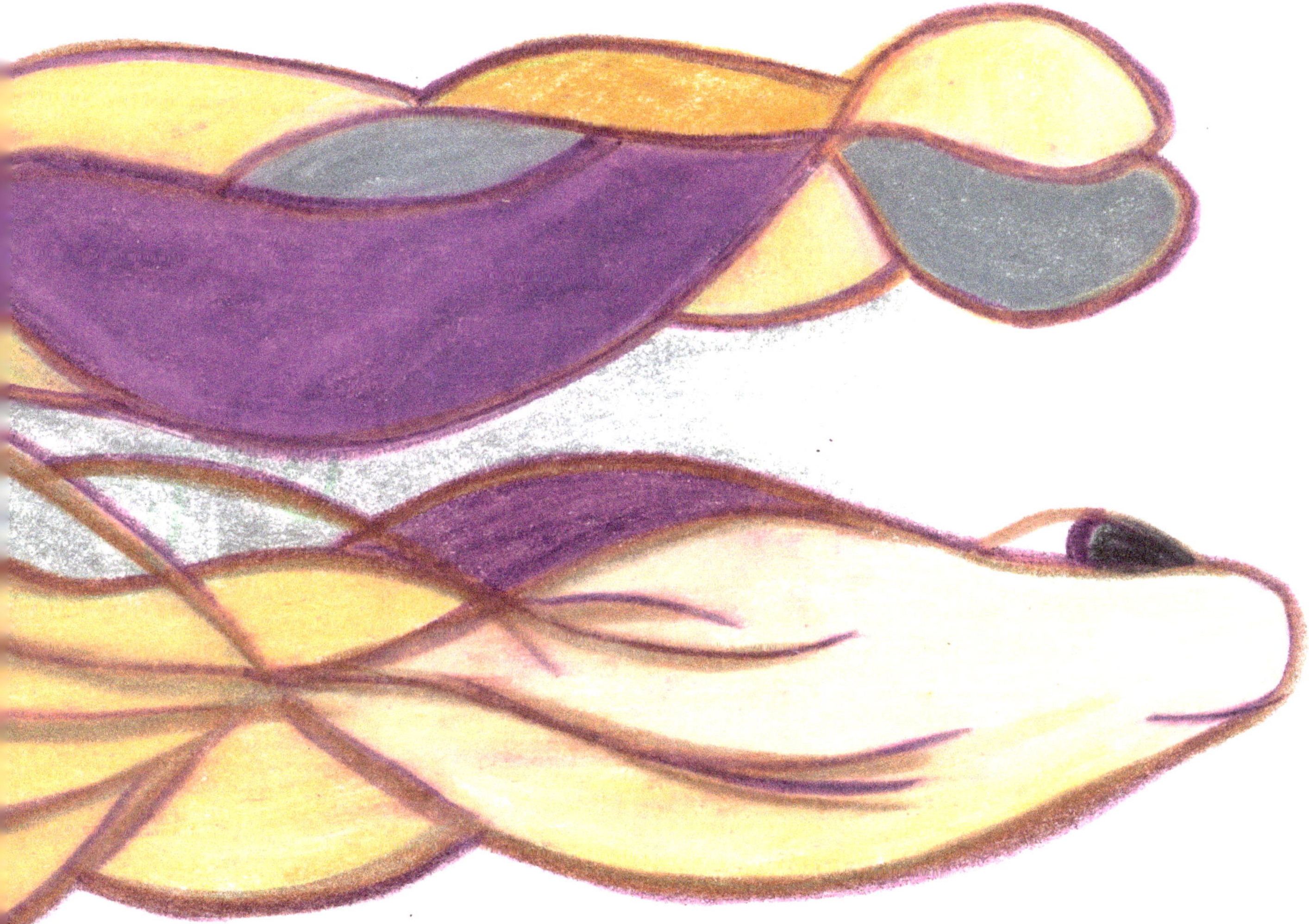

Try Vulnerability

1. Observe your breath for 10 minutes for 7 days. Rest post sessions.
2. Is keeping it secret harming you? Tell someone you trust if need be.
3. Blindfold yourself. Sit quietly for 10 minutes. Experience.
4. Prepare a speech. Invite a friend over. Stand up and deliver.
5. Sing in company. Loud. Record it.
6. Enrol in a class, something you know nothing about. Be uncertain.
7. Investigate a new place. Log your travels. Discover a new aspect of you.

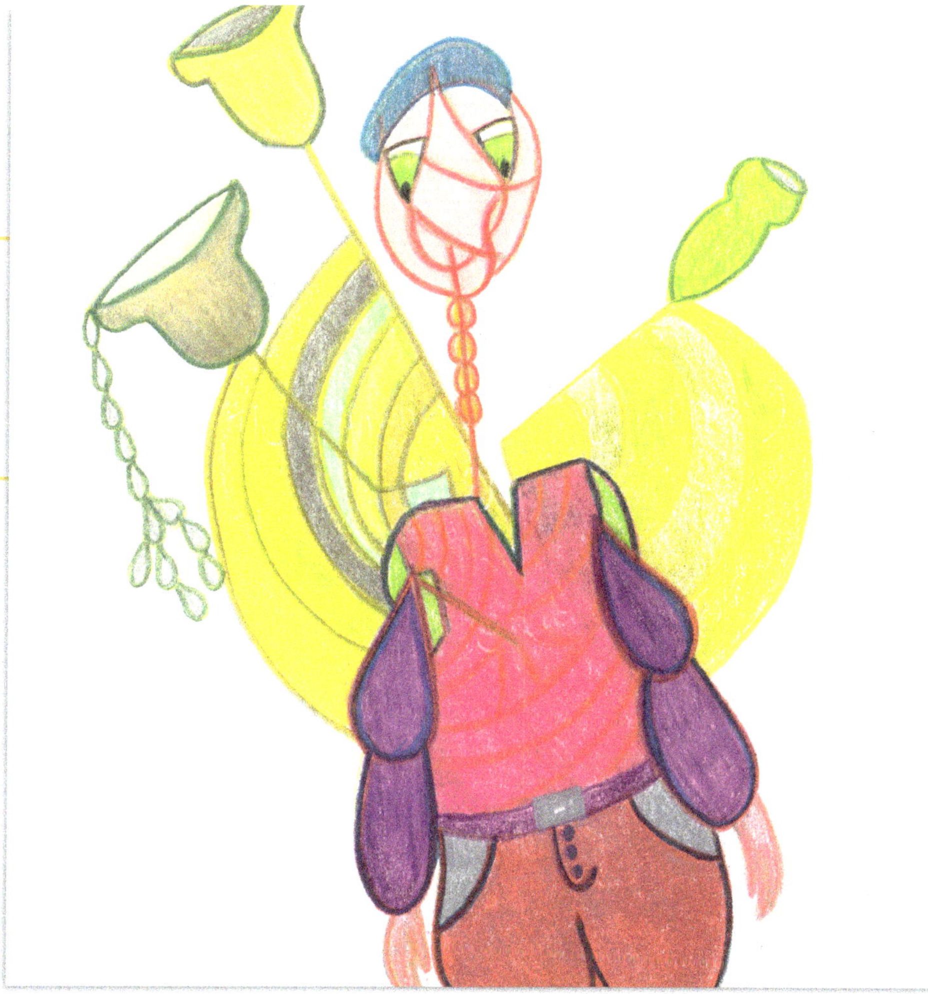

Extend Compassion

1. Observe your breath for 10 minutes for 7 days. Journal your thoughts for 10 minutes.
2. Can you still see what you value? No? Change position. Even a small step can alter the view.
3. Are you trivialising your life with too much chatter? Re-evaluate.
4. What could you lose today to make space for kindness?
5. What does the word "metanoia" mean? Journal. Interested?
6. Accept it as it is, not as you would like it to be. Saves time.
7. Wrap your arms around the mystery of another person. Be of comfort. Breathe.

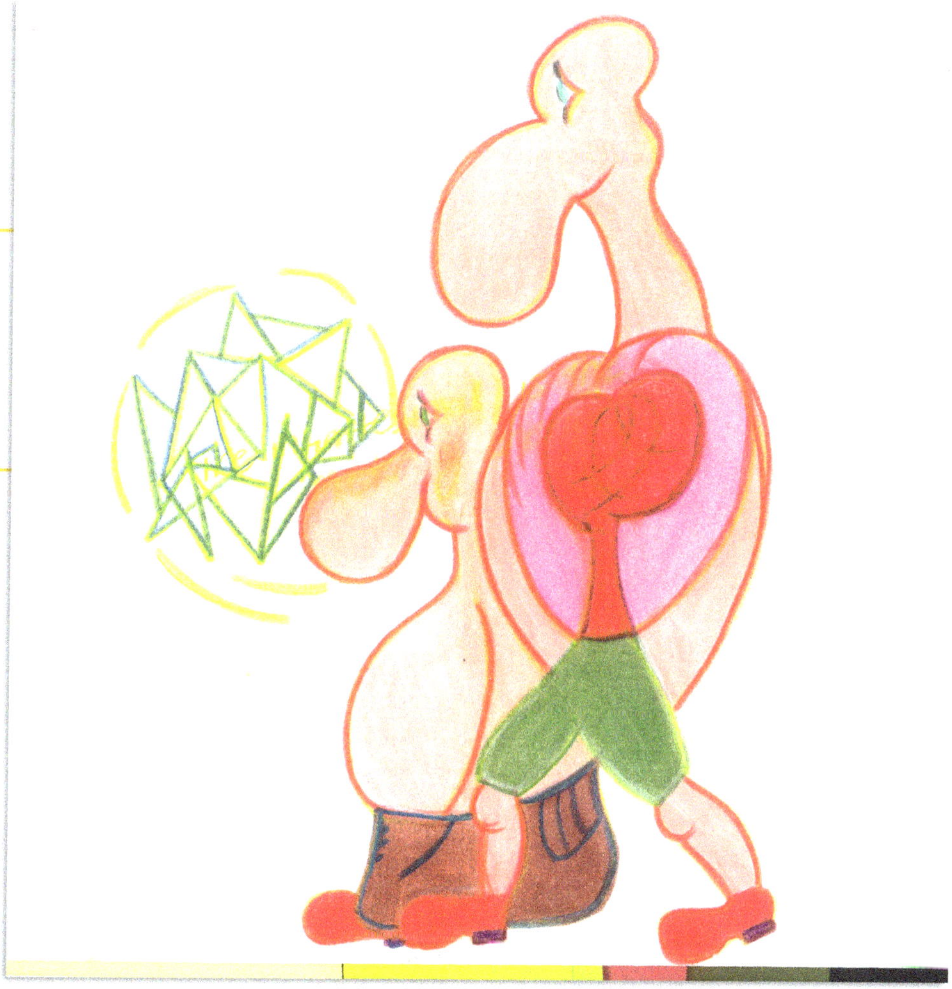

Expand Perception

1. Observe your breath for 10 minutes for 7 days. Keep your eyes shut and feel your face.
2. Get the other side of the story. Listen openly all the way to the end.
3. What is Dark Matter? Investigate. Based on your understanding tell someone about it.
4. Overturn comfort so you can learn something new. Wow! So many wonders.
5. Koinonia - Greek - to participate. How would you like to participate today?
6. What is EASE for you? How could you incorporate it today?
7. The way you pay attention to your life is how others will also. Want to change anything?

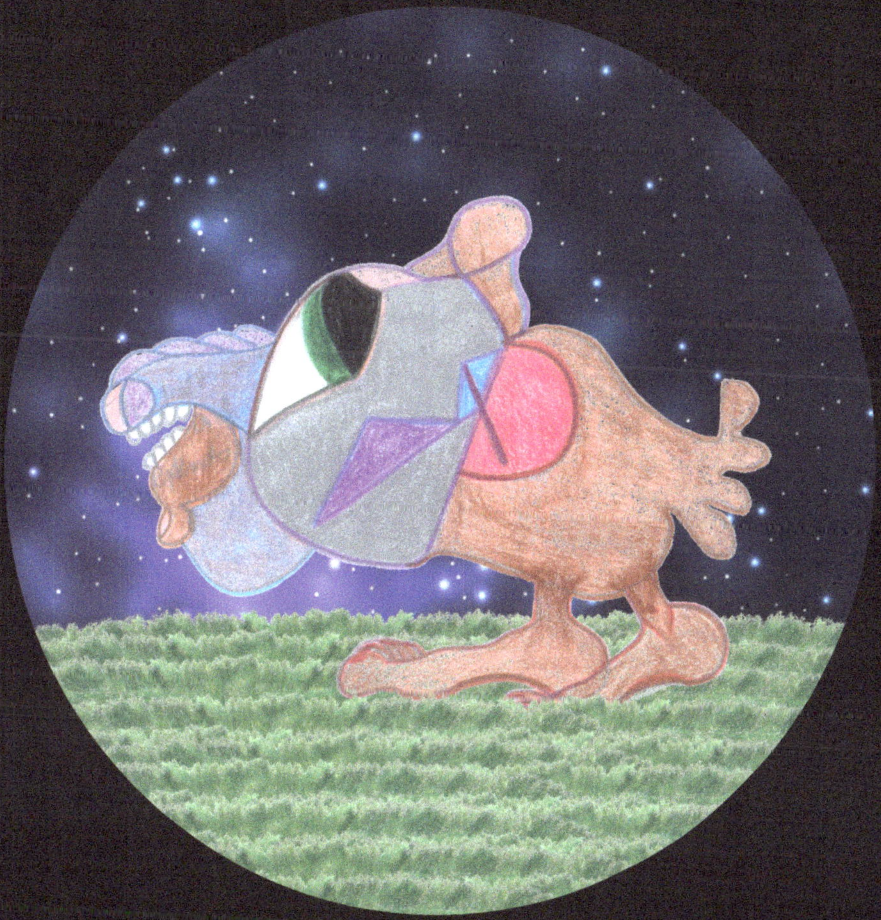

WEEK FORTY-FIVE

Remember

1. Observe your breath for 1 minute for 7 days. Does your body miss more time?

2. Visit a library online or in person. What subject matter is taking your attention?

3. What is your most legitimate purpose today? Continue.

4. Take a photo of yourself. Compare the image with Week 12 #1.

5. Record an event today. Write the whole story from the start, twice.

6. Draw a self portrait twice. Cut them up and collage a new aspect.

7. How do you want to be remembered? Write your own eulogy.

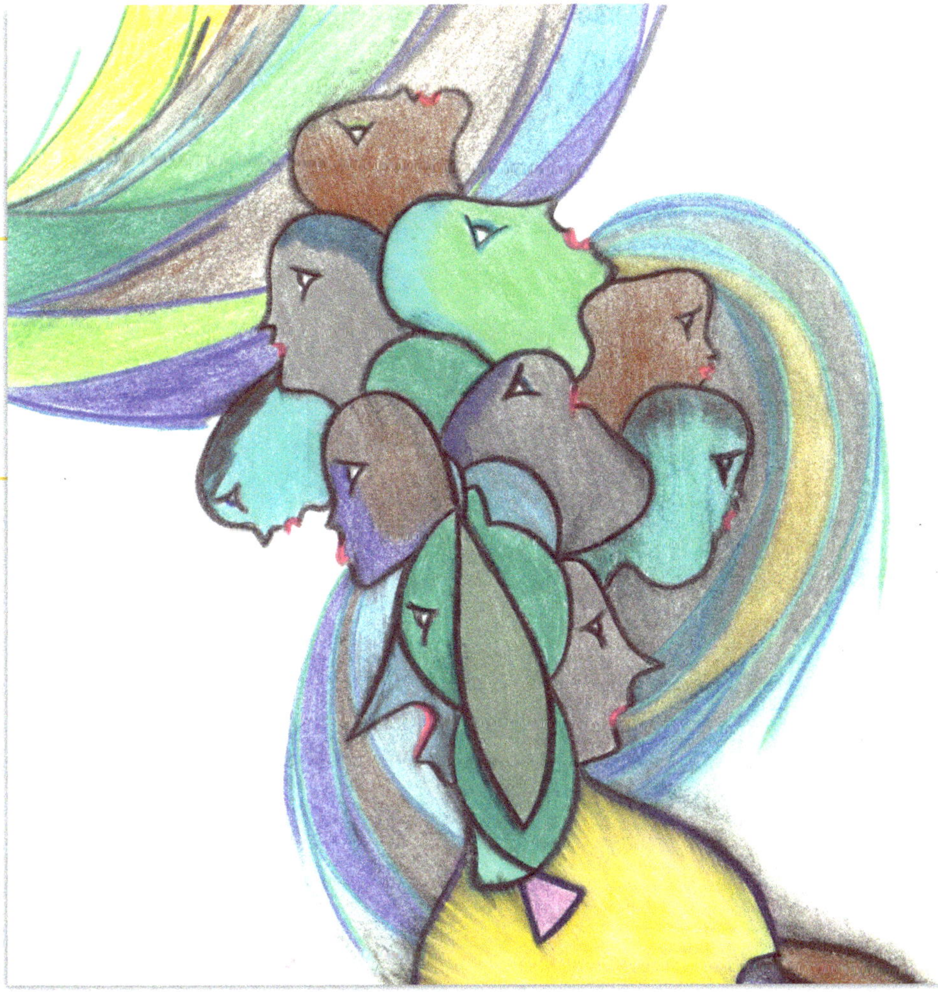

Communicate

1. Observe your breath for 5 minutes for 7 days. What bubbles to the surface?
2. To share. What does it mean? What can you share with others today?
3. Read a new poem. Allow the meaning to slowly permeate your being.
4. Write a new poem. Share your dreams in the language.
5. Watch a recording of an inspirational speech. What could you implement?
6. Words are events; they hold our experience. Choose words wisely today.
7. Draw or paint how you feel. Date, frame and gift to someone.

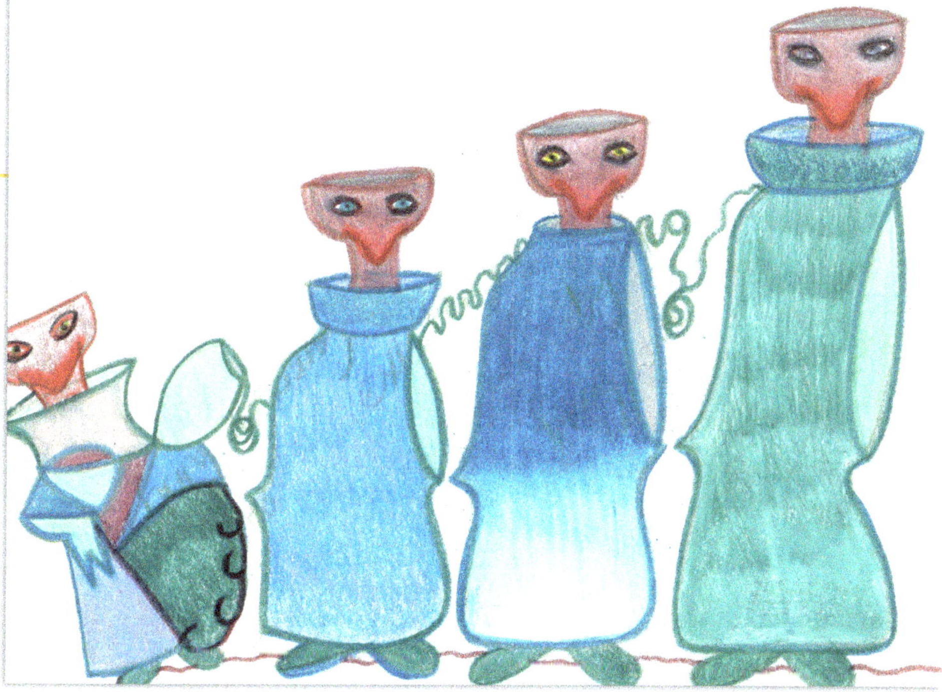

Forgive

1. Observe your breath for 10 minutes for 7 days. Are you offering friendship to yourself?
2. Have you fulfilled your expectation of yourself? There is still time. Giddy up.
3. Look upon the world with peaceful eyes today. What do you see?
4. Never give up. Never. Keep turning up. Most all of it depends on it.
5. How did you get here? Write the story up till now. Such wonders.
6. Visit a gallery. Find an image that encapsulates forgiveness. Photograph. Contemplate.
7. Draw your version of above image. Allow forgiveness to seep into it.

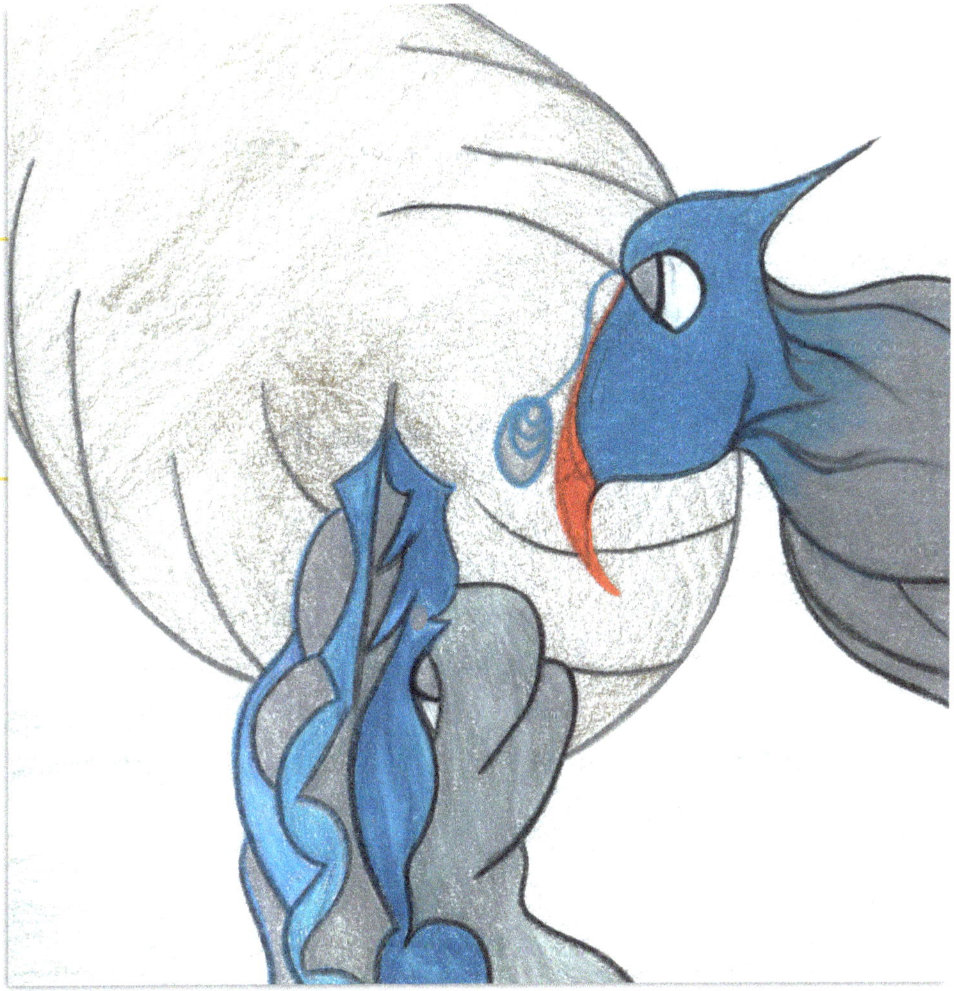

Embody Harmony

1. Be still for 20 minutes for 7 days. Be silent. Affirm this moment as part of the whole.
2. Are you being responsible for your own life? Claim it completely.
3. Make open time alone today without obligations. Be still and quiet.
4. Recall the event from Week 45 #5. Write it again today. Different?
5. What are you seeking? Draw your ideas. Exhibit in your space to consider.
6. Go out with yourself on a date. Just you.
7. Patience might be the antidote to anger? Experiment with this today.

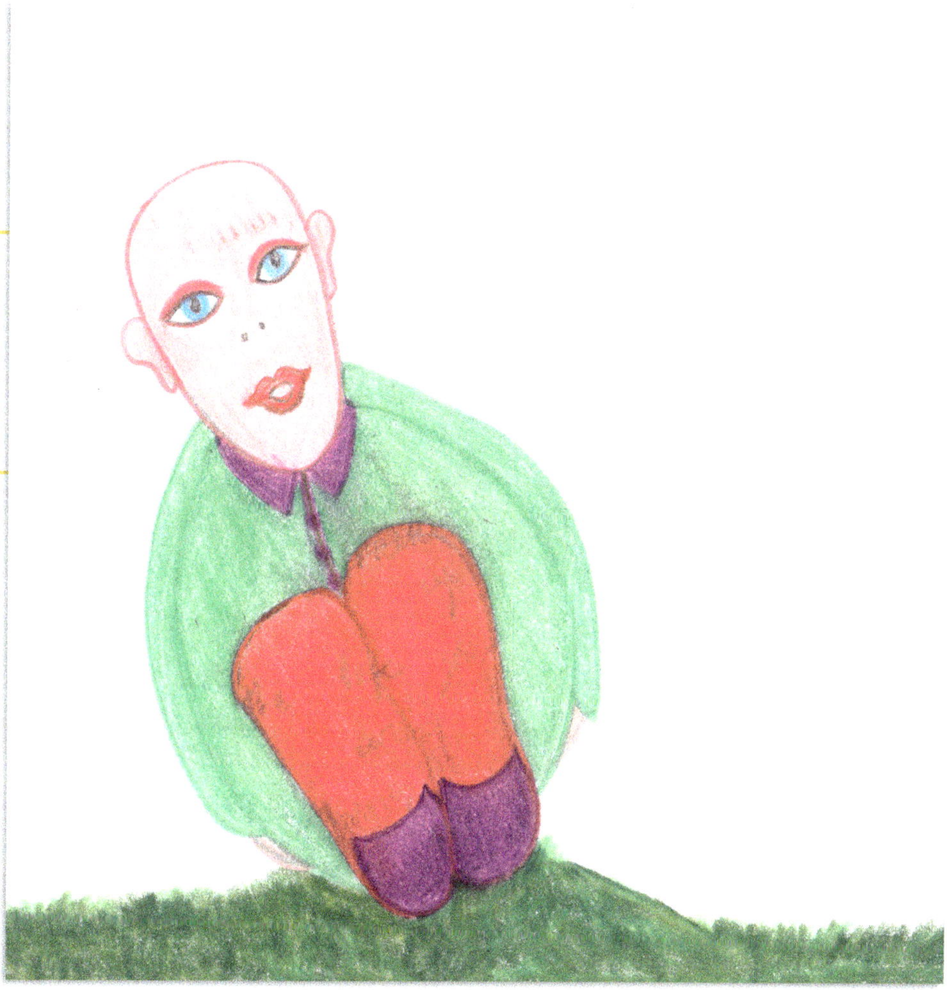

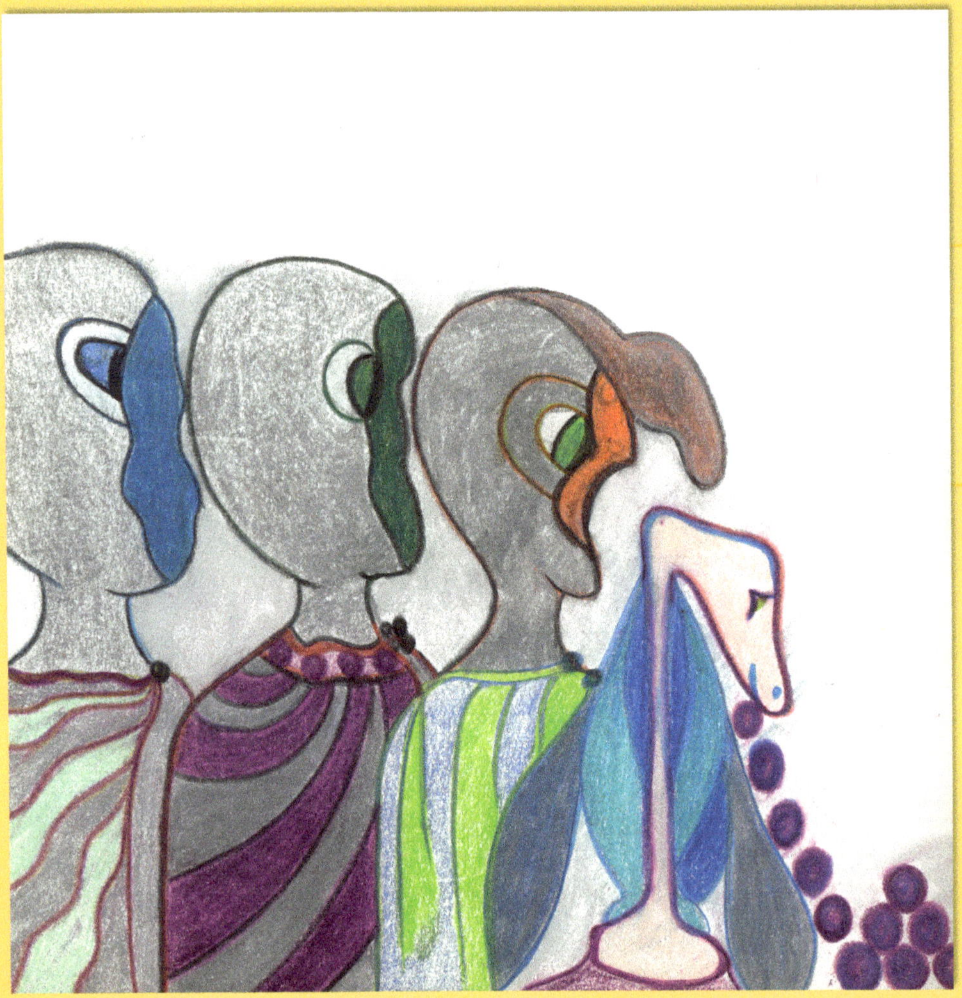

Educate

1. Observe your breath for 5 minutes for 7 days. What subject would you like to explore today?

2. What does it mean to have worth? Add ideas to your journal.

3. How can you employ healthy momentum today?

4. Educate: to lead out. Who can you lead out today? Maybe you?

5. Create a list of Great Questions and add to it each week. A store of provocations.

6. Uncover 7 new facts on a subject of your choice. Share discoveries.

7. Move your body dynamically every 30 minutes today for 2 minutes.

Meditate

1. Observe your breath for 10 minutes for 7 days. Draw your experience.

2. Walk early each day for 20 minutes without music. Stop and listen every few minutes.

3. Choose 6 styles of meditation to investigate. Experiment with one. *

4. Visit a gallery online or in person choose a painting, contemplate breathing in and out slowly.

5. You always have enough to give. So give.

6. Take a friend out for cake. Pay attention to your friend and cake.

7. Embrace your right to express and experience. Comparison kills creativity.

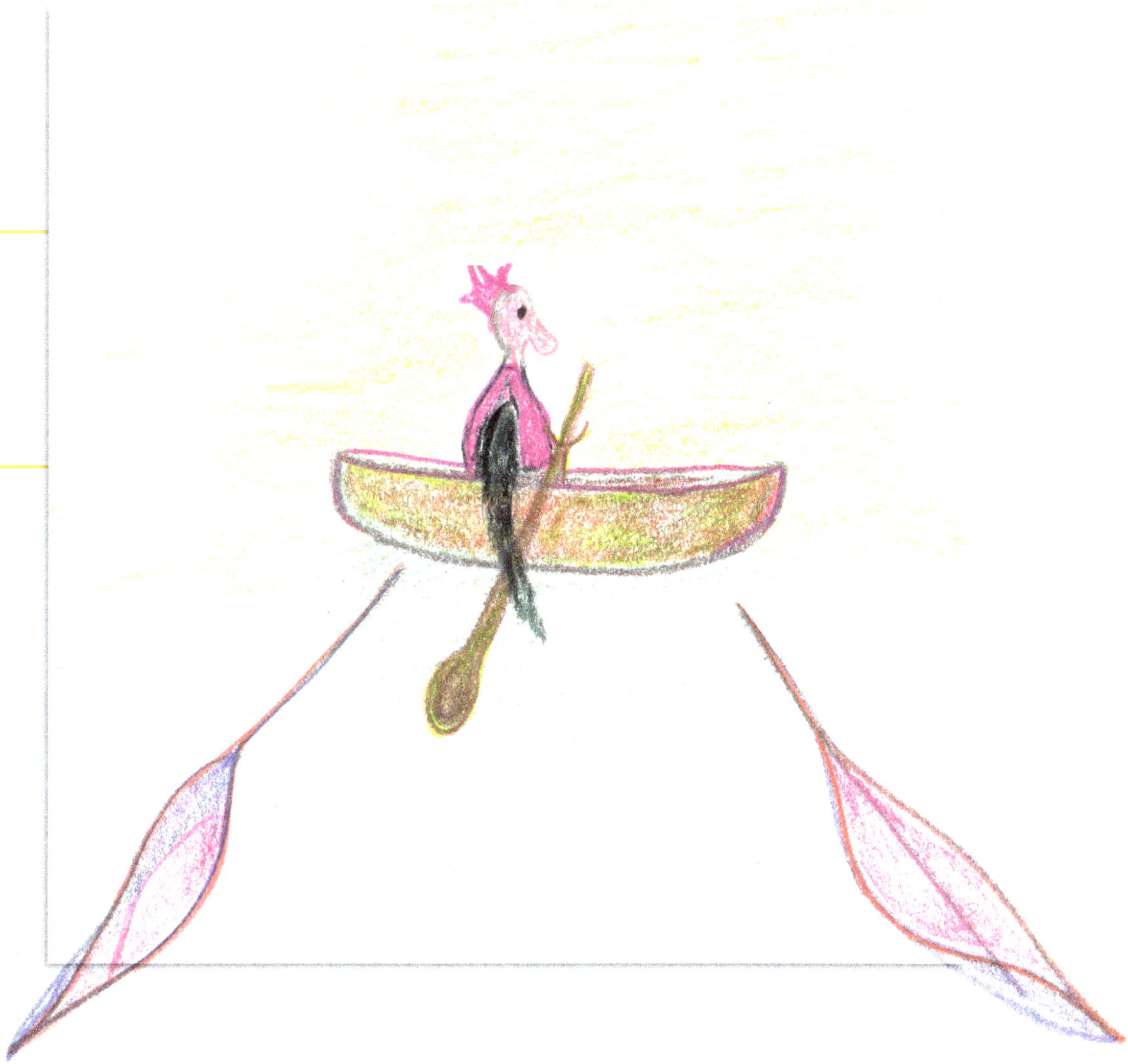

Spawn Art

1. Observe your breath for 10 minutes for 7 days. Imagine something you would like to make.

2. How might you carry yourself out beyond fear? What help is required?

3. What would your best friend tell you to do? So... do it.

4. Bring the outside inside.

5. Make art today that expresses your point of view. Gift to another.

6. Choose your favourite fruit. Create a still life using only one colour.

7. Go swimming. Submerge yourself in water.

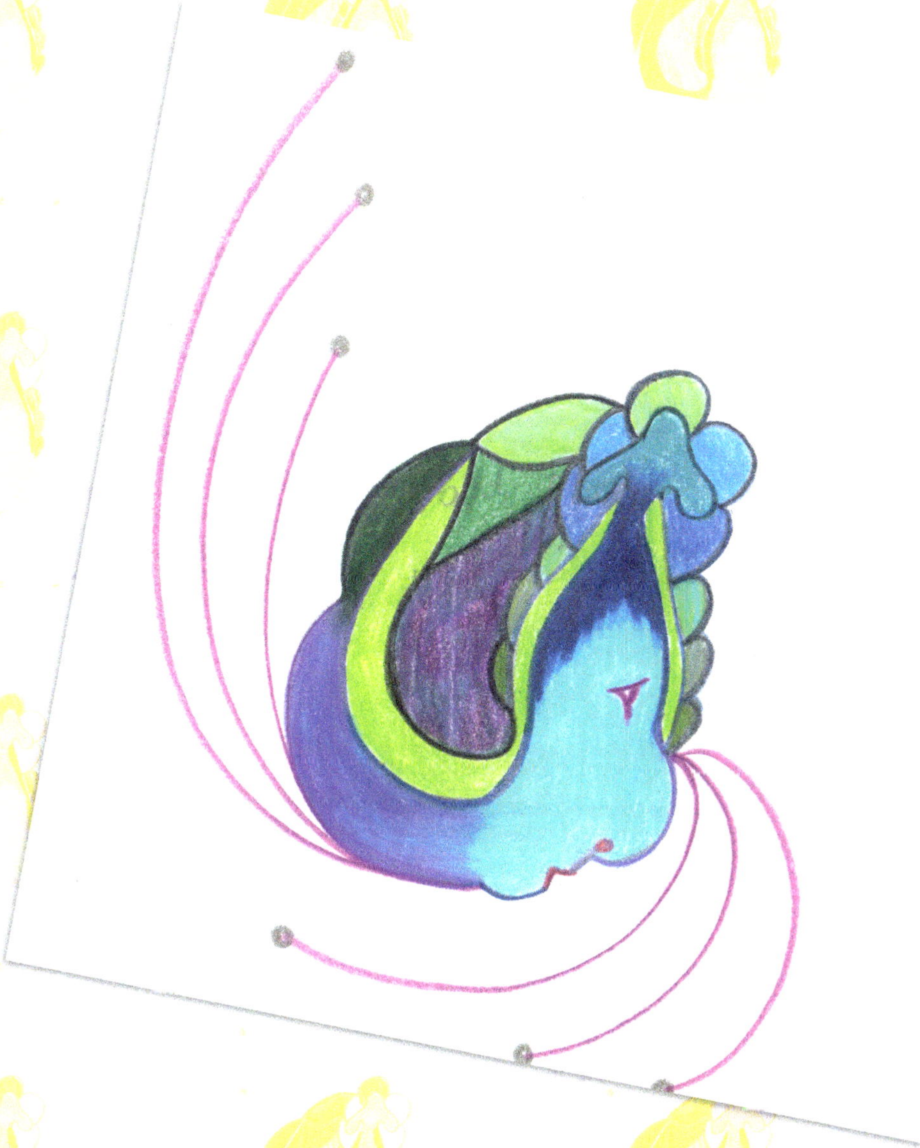

Create

1. Observe your breath for 10 minutes for 7 days. Wear a costume.
2. Celebrate today by observing beauty in any form for 10 minutes.
3. What could you add? What could you subtract? Does it need music?
4. Write the instruction you need for today. ACTION your life.
5. What are you glad of right now? Express it in any form today.
6. Disrupt your day your week your year. Go.
7. It is not personal and it is changing.
8. Turn up every day. Every single day. Set the example you want to follow.

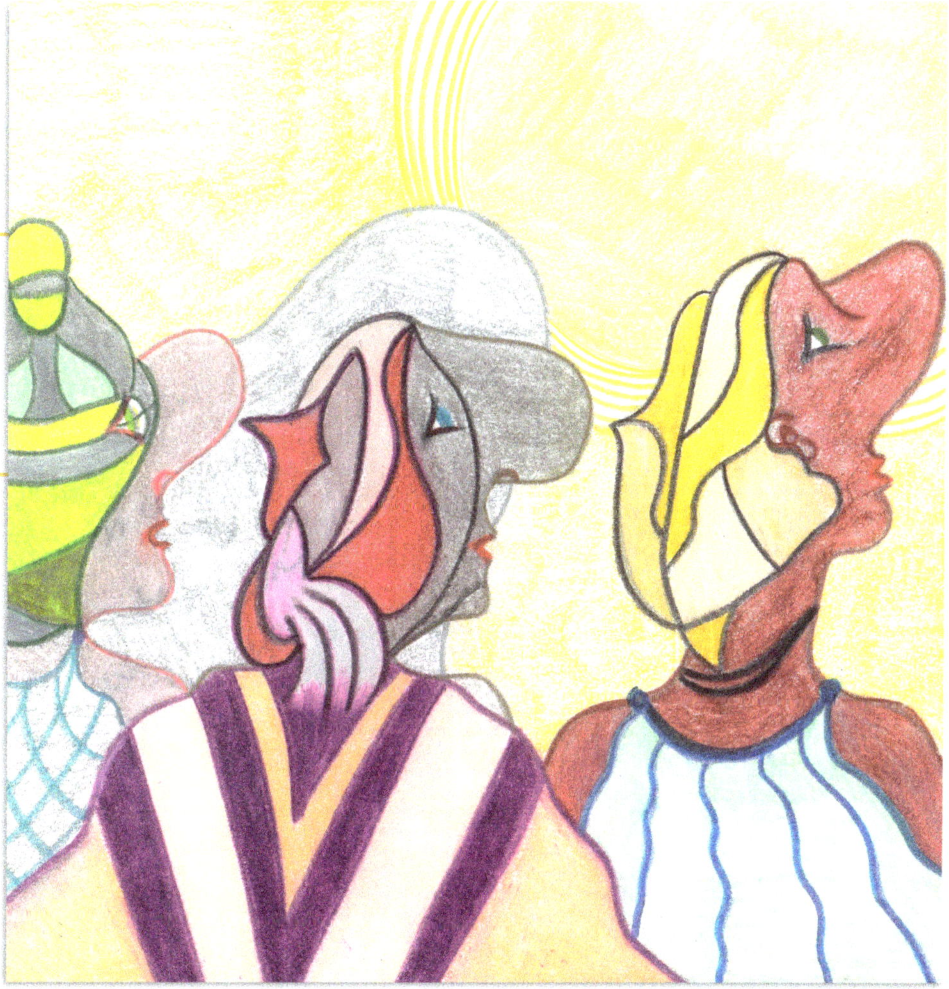

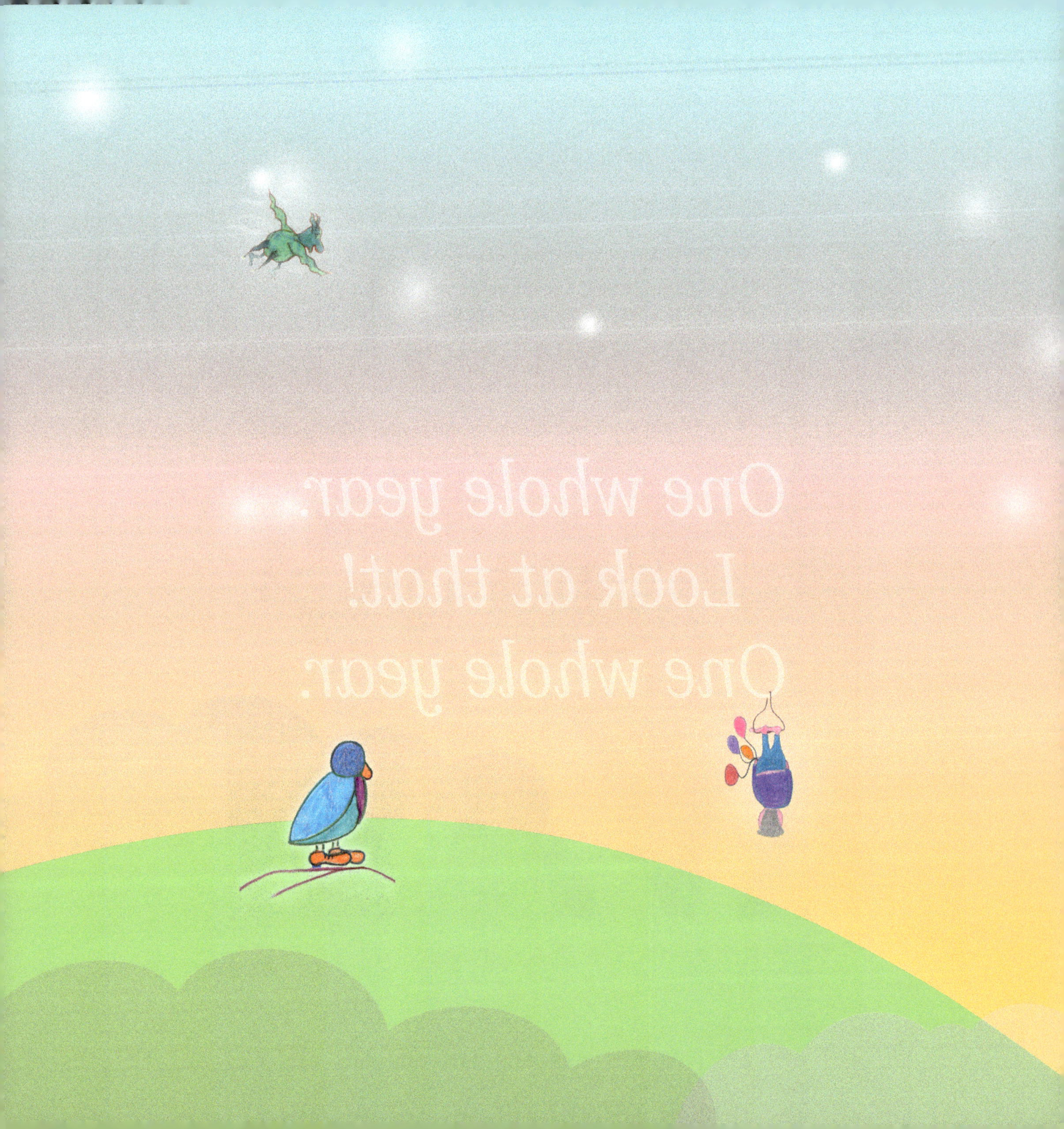

One whole year.
Look at that!
One whole year.

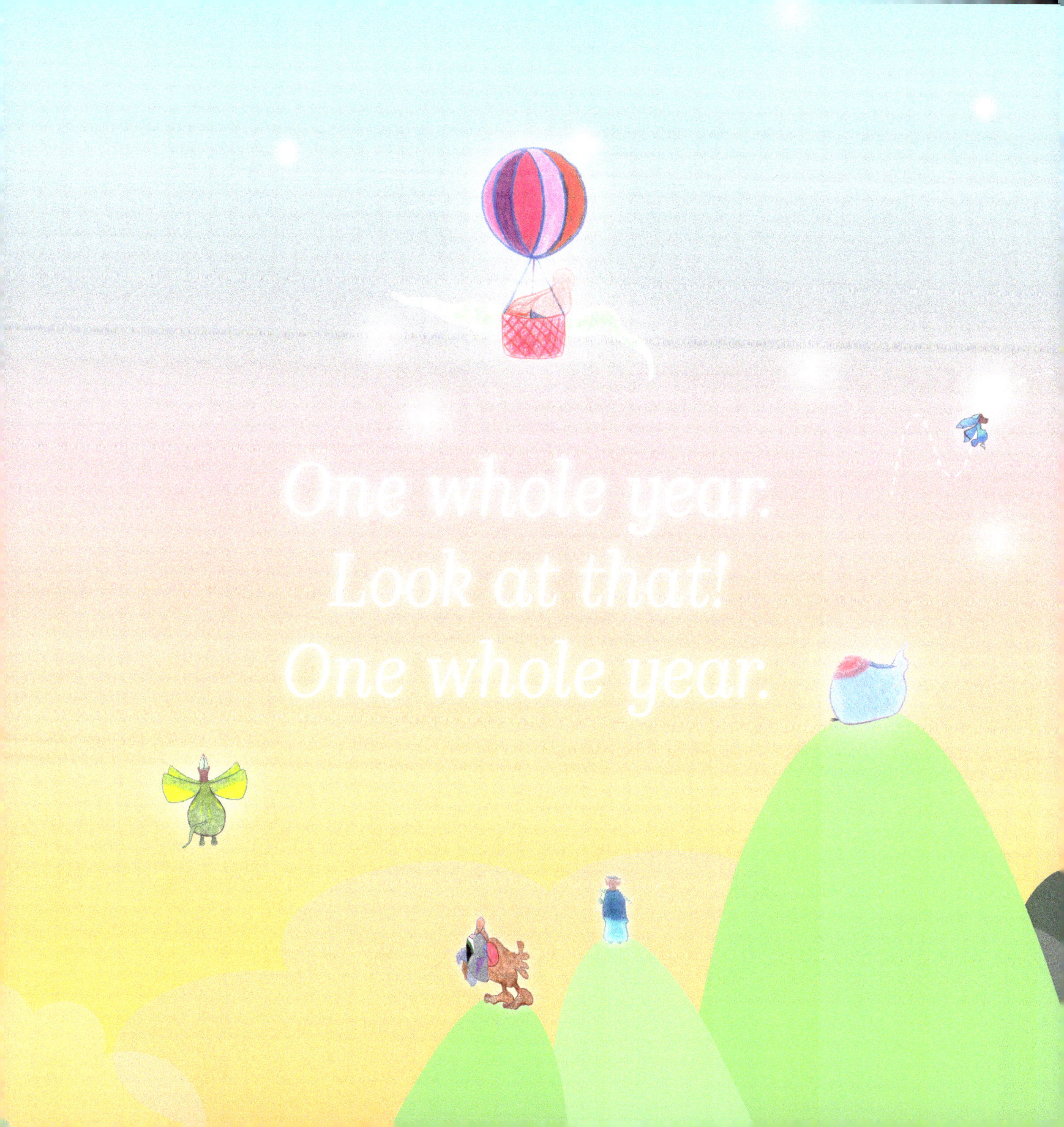

One whole year.
Look at that!
One whole year.

oh yes…

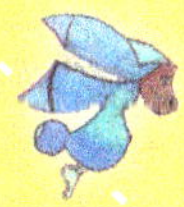

also...

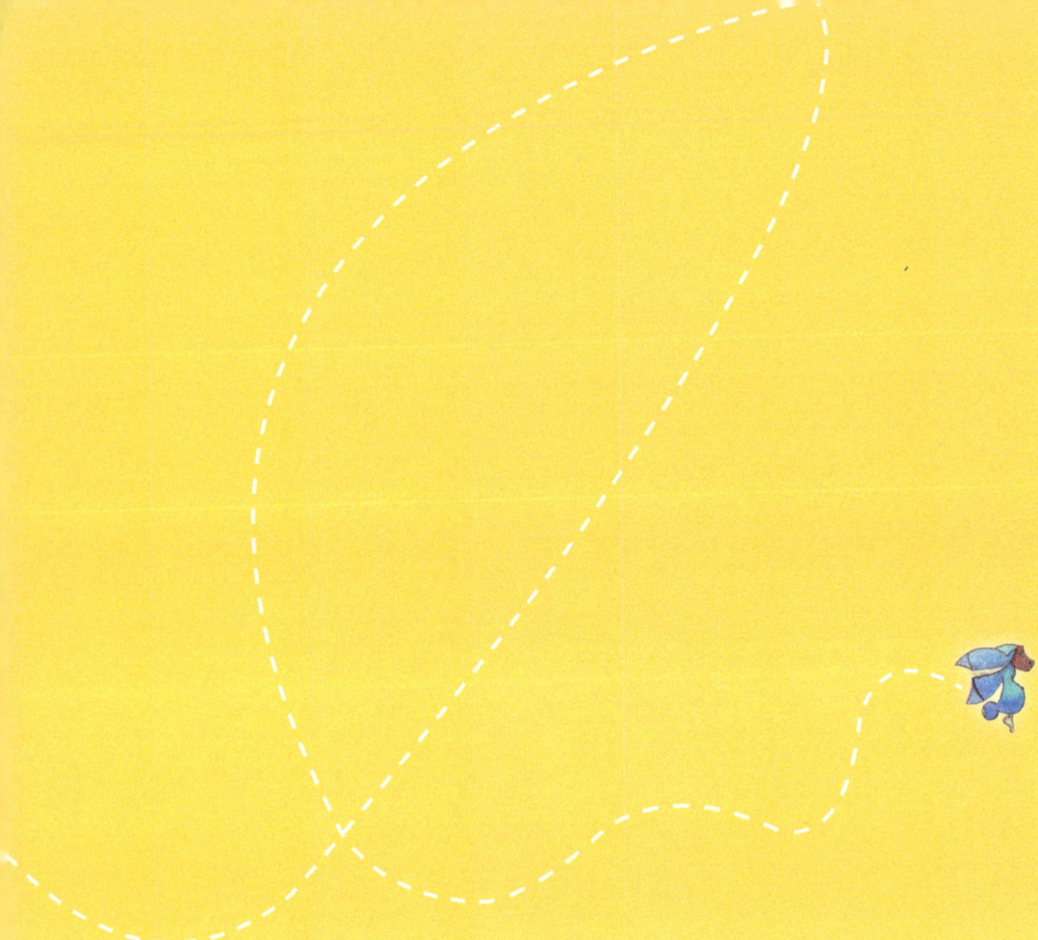

IN CASE OF LEAP YEAR

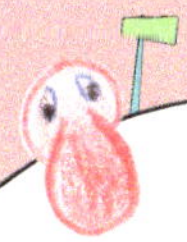

Day 366:
How might you
manifest
magic?
Jump in.

BREAK GLASS

BACK OF THE BOOK

Page 24 | Seek purpose

Week 3 Task #2 The memory you locate may be a thing: a photo, a drawing, a letter, a piece of jewellery, a toy, a certificate... Or it may be a memory or a song or smell or even a place. You will know what is right for you to locate yourself at that earlier time.

Page 26 | Foster will power

Week 4 Task #5 As suggested in the earlier note for those who have physical ailments, injuries or disabilities disallowing you from taking the stairs please devise a challenging physical task to allow the use of your body in a strenuous way to accommodate your physicality safely.

Week 4 Task #6 Suggestions for redeploying time saved: paint, sing, read, write, talk to a friend, sleep, daydream, dance, walk, swim, run, learn a language, go to a gallery, research an artist, make a list of new words to employ in conversation, garden, plan a trip, study something new, massage your feet, take a bath, write a short story... and on and on it goes. There are no limits to what you can achieve with this time.

Page 38 | En-joy

Week 10 Task #7 If you can't swing for any reason, lie down and visualise a swing with you on it. Swing as high as you can over and over for at least one minute. Feel the air rushing past your face, your hair streaming out behind you, let go a squeal of delight. Our spirits don't know the difference - they just know that something lovely is happening. Enjoy.

Page 78 | Surrender

Week 28 Task #5 You may have music you would like to listen to. Here's some more ideas:

- Nat Bartsch
- Nadje Noordhuis
- Peter Sculthorpe
- Michael Westlake
- Elena Kats-Chernin
- Sally Whitwell
- Mary Finsterer
- Margaret Sutherland
- Peggy Granville Hicks
- Liza Lim
- Brett Dean
- Deborah Cheetham
- Carl Vine
- William Barton
- Miriam Hyde
- Luke Howard
- Hildegard von Bingen
- Barbara Strozzi
- Louise Farrenc
- Clara Schumann
- Francesca Caccini
- Fanny Mendelssohn
- Isabella Leonarda
- Lili Boulanger
- Phamie Gow
- Debbie Wiseman
- Brahms
- Massenet
- Henryk Górecki
- Sibelius
- Erik Satie
- Alan Hovhaness
- Morton Feldman
- Claude Debussy

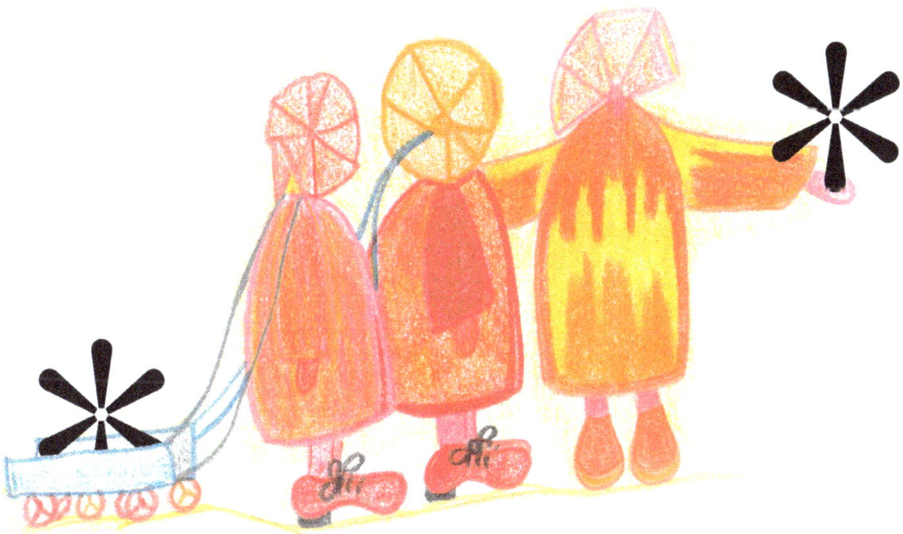

Page 82 | Give

Week 30 Task #1 Read inspiring material post your breath observation. This material can be anything from any field of enquiry that propels you into feeling uplifted, awed, encouraged, emboldened, exhilarated, heartened, mentally expanded or challenged, or inflamed to action. You are looking to enrich your mind and your intelligence.

Page 100 | Discover peace

Week 39 Task #7 Proud Flesh was a discovery via a Jane Hirshfield poem, titled 'For What Binds Us.'

Page 104 | Pay attention

Week 40 Task #7 You can refer to the previous list of possible music choices for your pleasure or allow them to take you off on a tangent of your own.

Page 124 | Meditate

Week 50 Task #3 The field of possible meditation styles is vast and open to interpretation depending on how and in what form you are using it. Our suggestion is to begin simply and follow what feels right for you. There are apps for your phone and various retreats and classes that you can attend to gain knowledge directly. Some meditation modes are related to religious or philosophical schools of thought which you may also be interested in investigating.

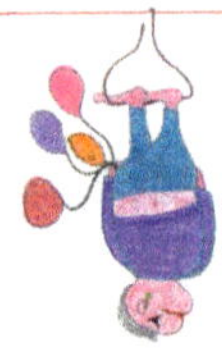

THE MAKERS

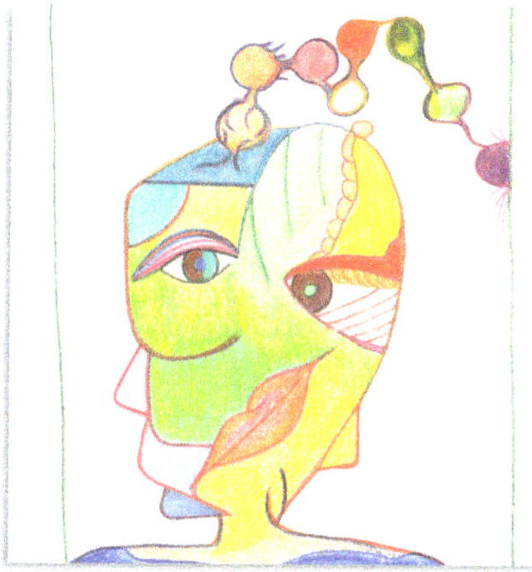

Georgina Capper is a creative who enjoys performing, writing, photographing and designing. Surprised on more than one occasion by the thought that each day led to this one, she's excited to see where this one will lead. Many years ago she studied German literature and while these days much of the language eludes her, Georgina occasionally may be heard singing a little Brecht auf Deutsch in the shower because why not.

Portrait by Louise

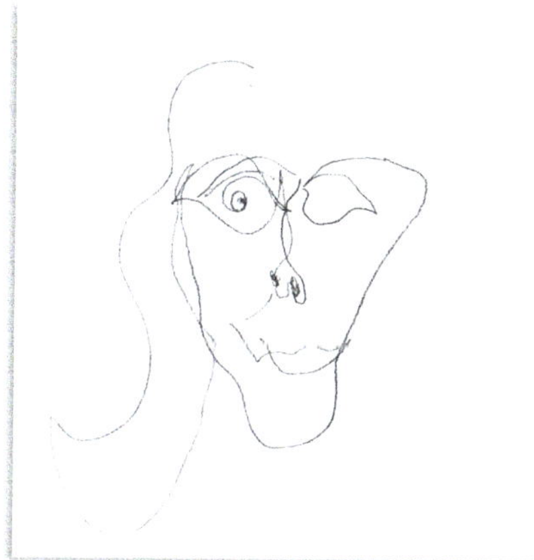

Louise Siversen is an actress amongst various other incarnations depending on the day and the time. She had threatened to write a book some day and now with her Brecht singing friend she has achieved it which only goes to show nothing is impossible. Louise is a great believer in build it and they will come, or at least mill about for a while. She also firmly believes that if it doesn't exist then you could just make it...

Portrait by Georgina